WINING & DINING

PARIS

by Andy Herbach
& Karl Raaum

Authors of *Open Road's Best of Paris*
and *Eating & Drinking in Paris*

OPEN ROAD PUBLISHING

www.openroadguides.com

Copyright © 2014 by Andy Herbach & Karl Raaum
ISBN 13: 978-1-59360-195-9
Library of Congress Control Number: 2014937053

See page 133 for Acknowledgments, About the Authors, and Photo Credits

CONTENTS.

MAPS

Note: There is an arrondissement map at the beginning of each section.

1. INTRODUCTION

When you think of Paris, what comes to mind? The Champs-Elysées? Montmartre? The Left Bank? For us, it's the fabulous wine and food we always find there.

That's because there's nowhere else on earth offering such a sensory celebration of food and wine. There's nowhere else on earth with a greater number of dining and drinking establishments per square mile to choose from. And, for some, there's absolutely nowhere else on earth one can feel more intimidated, trying to order something delicious to eat or drink.

In the last few years, wine bars have popped up all over Paris, changing the way Parisians and tourists alike experience food and wine. No more unwieldy, leather-bound wine lists to wrestle with! Instead, you'll find casual places serving small plates and featuring interesting wines from small vineyards.

We've included Paris's best restaurants, wine bars, wine shops, cafes, bistros, champagne bars and more – making your wining and dining decisions a snap.

We've included both the newest offerings as well as a number of lovely old restaurants and bistros, many of which have survived and flourished for more than one hundred years. Make a point of dining in at least one of these historic settings to experience the culinary heritage of this great city.

Wining and Dining in Paris was created for those of you who want to truly experience the extraordinary food and wine the city has to offer, keeping travelers – like us – returning again and again.

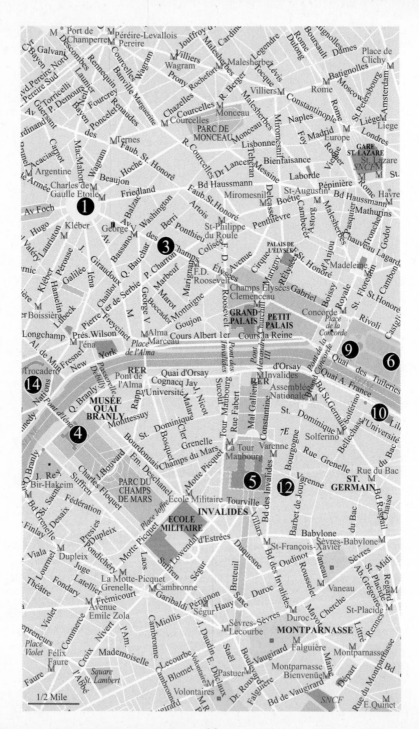

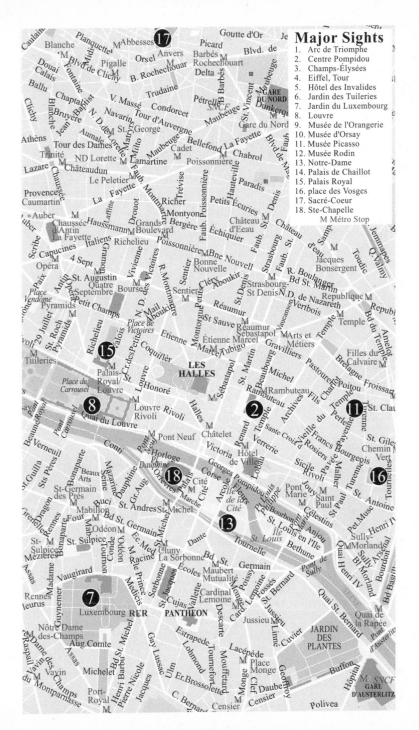

Major Sights

1. Arc de Triomphe
2. Centre Pompidou
3. Champs-Élysées
4. Eiffel, Tour
5. Hôtel des Invalides
6. Jardin des Tuileries
7. Jardin du Luxembourg
8. Louvre
9. Musée de l'Orangerie
10. Musée d'Orsay
11. Musée Picasso
12. Musée Rodin
13. Notre-Dame
14. Palais de Chaillot
15. Palais Royal
16. place des Vosges
17. Sacré-Coeur
18. Ste-Chapelle

M Métro Stop

Paris Arrondissements

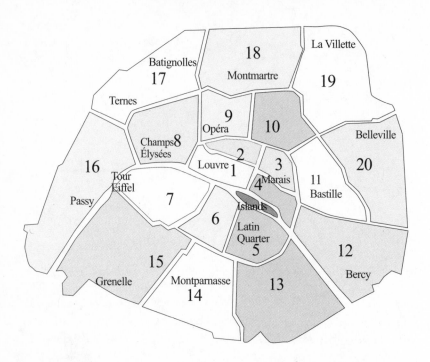

BONUS SIGHTS SECTIONS IN THIS BOOK

Even though this is a book about the extraordinary wine and food Paris has to offer, what are you going to be doing when you're not wining and/or dining? Sightseeing, of course! And because Paris has many wonderful sights to see, we've begun each *arrondissement* with the best that district has to offer—just a little bonus to go with your free-range veal and *vin rouge*!

2. RESTAURANT BASICS

PARIS

Paris is the most fabulous city in the world, not because of the Eiffel Tower or the Champs-Élysées, but because there's simply no other place in the world like it.

It's called the City of Light, but perhaps it should be called the City of Promise. Around every corner is the promise of another beautiful street, another bistro filled with people eating delicious food (Paris is a city where you have to work at having a bad meal), another building that in any other city would be remarkable, but in Paris is just another building. Walk down practically any block in Paris, and the sights, smells and sounds will excite you. Paris has changed since we began traveling here. It's cleaner, healthier (no more smoke-filled restaurants and much more healthier dining alternatives), and friendlier (the rude Parisian is a thing of the past, although we have never experienced a rude Parisian).

Wining and dining in Paris is not just eating a meal. It is experiencing a tradition of dining that exists nowhere else. *Wining and Dining in Paris* was made for those who want to *savor* food and wine at its finest.

WINING & DINING IN PARIS

Food in Paris is, for the most part, superb. We suspect this is one of the main reasons you've come here! You will find fantastic cuisine and great wine if you follow the suggestions in this book.

WHAT AM I EATING ... OR DRINKING?
To help you decipher menus written in French, get *Eating & Drinking in Paris*. It has a comprehensive menu translator, restaurant reviews, and is written by me!

PRICES
Prices are for a main course and without wine. Our price key is as follows:

- Inexpensive: under €10
- Moderate: €11–20
- Expensive: €21–30
- Very Expensive: over €31

Lunch, even at the most expensive restaurants listed below, always has a lower fixed price. Credit cards accepted unless noted.

A FEW POINTERS
No other city in the world has a greater number of places to eat per square mile than Paris. Nowhere else can you find the variety, the charm, the sheer joy of dining. And nowhere else can you be more intimidated, trying to get fed. Parisians observe all kinds of decorum about their food. They eat in a nearly ritualistic manner, and want you to do so as well. As travelers we feel we are often blundering into a private party and haven't received all the pertinent information. The following is some of that information.

THE MENU

A *menu* is a **fixed-price meal**, not that piece of paper listing the food items. **If you want what we consider a menu**, you need to ask for *la carte*. The menu is almost always posted on the front of the restaurant so you know what you're getting into, both foodwise and pricewise, before you enter. The **fixed-price daily menu** (*menu fixe*) will generally include several choices for each of 2 or 3 courses. The daily fixed-price menu is cheaper than ordering off the menu (carte). Our American term à la carte means 'of the menu,' in case you hadn't noticed.

Restaurants frequently offer a **plate of the day** (*plat du jour*), and some restaurants offer a **set-price gourmet menu** (*menu dégustation*) of specialties of the chef. The price of a meal will occasionally include the **house wine** (*vin compris*).

A simple **green salad** (*salade verte*) is occasionally served with or sometimes after the main course, before the cheese course or dessert. Rarely is this type of salad even listed on the menu. Larger, more involved – and to us what seem like full meals–salads such as roquefort, lardons and endive – are usually listed as first courses or entrées. However, times have changed and you may now order a green salad as an appetizer but you will most likely have to ask for it, because, as we said earlier, you won't find it on the menu.

An *entrée* is a **first course**, the *plat* is the **main course**, followed by cheese and then dessert. Coffee is served at the end – never with your meal. There are all sorts of coffees that you can order decaffeinated which, if your meal is ending at midnight as so often happens in Paris, you might want to consider. Ask for *déca* which rhymes with day-cah.

TIPS ON BUDGET DINING

There's no need to spend a lot of money in Paris to have good food. Of course it hurts when the dollar is weaker than the euro, but there are all kinds of fabulous foods to be had inexpensively all over Paris.

Eat at a neighborhood restaurant or bistro. The menu, with prices, is posted in the window. Never order anything whose price is not known in advance.

If you see *selon grosseur* (sometimes abbreviated as *s/g*), this means that you're paying by weight, which can be extremely expensive. Avoid restaurants and bistros with English menus.

Delis and food stores can provide cheap and wonderful meals. Buy some cheese, bread, wine and other snacks and have a picnic in one of Paris's great parks.

Lunch, even at the most expensive restaurants listed in this guide, always has a lower fixed price. So, have lunch as your main meal.

Large department stores frequently have supermarkets (in the basement) and restaurants that have reasonably priced food. And street vendors generally sell inexpensive, terrific food.

For the cost of a cup of coffee or a drink, you can linger at a café and watch the world pass you by for as long as you want.

HISTORIC RESTAURANTS

Recognized for its food traditions the world over, Paris is filled with restaurants and bistros – many of which have survived and flourished for over one hundred years. Make a point of dining in at least one of these historic settings to experience the culinary heritage of this great city.

WHY IS THERE A DOG AT THE TABLE NEXT TO ME?

Parisians really love their dogs. It is not uncommon (no matter what type of eating establishment you are dining in) to find several dogs under tables, or even on their own chairs.

ASKING FOR YOUR BILL

The **bill in a restaurant** is called *l'addition*...but the **bill in a bar** is called *le compte* or *la note*; confusing? It's easier if you just make a scribbling motion with your fingers on the palm of your hand.

TIPPING

A **service charge** is almost always added to your bill in Paris. Depending on the service, it is sometimes appropriate to leave an additional 5 to 10%. The menu will usually note that service is included (*service compris*). Sometimes this is abbreviated with the letters *s.c.* The letters *s.n.c.* stand for *service non compris*; this means that the **service is not included** in the price, and you must leave a tip.

You will sometimes find *couvert* or **cover charge** on your menu (a small charge just for placing your butt at the table).

MEALTIMES

In Paris, lunch is served from noon to around 2:00 p.m., and dinner from 8:00 p.m. to 11:00 p.m. Restaurants usually have two seatings: at 8:00 or 8:30 p.m., and at 10:00 or 10:30 p.m. The restaurant will be less crowded at the early seating, but don't worry, it will fill up fast.

RESERVATIONS

It's advisable if you're visiting a restaurant (as opposed to a bistro or café) to have reservations. Although you might see an empty restaurant and assume there will be seats available, most places we have listed will be full by 8:00 p.m. – with people who have made reservations. We advise making reservations in person.

We like to do a walk-by in the afternoon, stop in and make reservations. Don't be afraid. The word for reservation is the same in English and French. You can do times and numbers with your fingers. If you speak a little French, you can do it on the phone. The problem with phoning, however, comes when, after you've said in a timid voice that you would like to make reservations if possible, they ask you a question in rapid-fire French and at that pace asking what your name is sounds pretty much like how many people are in the party or what time were you thinking about eating. Be patient; eventually you'll get the idea across.

Phone numbers, days closed and hours of operation often change, so it's advisable to check ahead. Restaurants in tourist areas may have different hours and days of operation during low season. Reservations are recommended for all restaurants unless noted. The telephone country code for France is 33. When calling within France you must dial the area code. The area code for Paris is 01. However, you do not use the 0 before the area code when calling France from the U.S. or Canada. Confused? Here's what it looks like: From the United States: (011) 33 1/43.26.48.23. From within Paris: 01/43.26.48.23.

WATER

Europeans joke that you can tell a U.S. tourist from his fanny pack, clothes and ubiquitous bottle of mineral water. Tap water is safe in Paris. Occasionally, you will find *non potable* signs in restrooms. This means that the water is not safe for drinking.

Waiters and waitresses sometimes bring *eau minérale* (mineral water) to your table. You will be charged for it, so if you don't want mineral water ask for *une carafe d'eau* or *eau du robinet* (tap water).

TYPES OF EATING ESTABLISHMENTS

We think of most of these places as restaurants. We have a hard time seeing the differences between many of these establishments. Cafés seem like bars, bistros seem like brasseries, and they all seem like restaurants. What some people think of as a limited menu can seem complete to someone else (like us). Our full list of restaurants includes cafés, brasseries, bistros, restaurants and wine bars.

Alimentation: A small food store.

Auberge: An inn serving food and drink. These are most often found in the country, but restaurants in Paris also use the name.

Bar à café: Coffee shop serving light meals. Don't be misled by the name, though, as they rarely serve alcohol.

Bistro: Smaller and less fashionable than a restaurant, serving traditional, simple French food. Some are very similar to taverns or pubs.

Bar à champagne: Champagne bar.

Bar à vin: Wine bar.

Boucherie: Butcher's shop.

Boulangerie: Bakery. Nowhere else on earth can you get baguettes that taste like they do in France. Bread is often offered bien cuit (crusty)or bien tendre (doughy). Many boulangeries also sell sandwiches, tarts, quiches and small pizzas.

Brasserie: Originally, this term referred to a beer hall, but today serves food and drink.

Buffet: Eating establishment usually found in railroad stations.

Cabaret: Dinner and a show.

Café: Simple café dining is one of the pleasures of a trip to Paris. You can learn more sitting in a café for an hour than spending the day in a museum. In Paris, people-watching is like no other place in the world. Cafés serve alcoholic beverages and snacks. Some serve complete meals.

Cave: Cellar. This also refers to a wine shop. See Vins et Alcools.

Charcuteries: Originally these were pork butchers selling pork, ham, sausages, jambon de Paris and sometimes chicken. Now, most are delicatessens with prepared salads, quiches and other food tarts.

Chevaline: Horse-meat butcher's shop. These shops are becoming few and far between, but have a small and devoted clientele. Usually, there is a horse-head emblem on the front of the shop.

Chocolaterie: Chocolate shop.

Confiserie: Sweet shop.

Crémerie: Cream (and cheese) shop.

Crêperies: Popular for lunch, serving crêpes (thin filled pancakes).

Emporter: Carry-out foods.

Épicerie: Grocer's shop (literally "spice shop").

Express: Any establishment with this name is usually a snack bar.

Fromagerie: Serves up to 400 official types of cheese.

Glaces et Sorbets/Glacier: Ice cream and sorbet shop.

Hostellerie: Upscale country restaurant.

Marché: Market.

Marchand de Légumes: Vegetable shop.

Pâtisseries: Pastry shops.

Pizzerias: You can figure this one out yourself.

Poissonnerie: Seafood shop.

Relais: Country inn or restaurant.

Restaurant: See our separate section on recommended restaurants.

Restoroute: Restaurant found on the highway.

Rôtisserie: Restaurant that usually specializes in roasted and grilled meats, especially chicken.

Salon de Thé: Open mid-morning to late evening, serving light fare, salads, cakes, ice cream and, of course, *thé* (tea).

Tabac: Bars where you can also buy cigarettes (they are, in fact, the only places in France where you can buy tobacco), stamps, tickets for public transportation, lottery tickets and phone cards. They are often also cafés.

Traiteur: Delicatessen (this can also mean caterer).

Triperie: Tripe shop.

Vins et Alcools: Wine and liquor shop.

Volailler: Poultry shop.

FOOD MARKETS & OTHER PLACES TO FIND FOOD

Food markets are very interesting. Though you may feel intimidated by the wild goings-on (not to mention the sights and smells) it is absolutely worth a trip to see a real **outdoor Parisian market**. Filled with colorful vendors, stinky cheese, fresh produce, poultry and hanging rabbits, this is real Paris at its most diverse and beautiful. Parisians still shop (some every day) at food markets around the city. Unless noted otherwise, all are open Tuesday through noon on Sunday. Some of the best-known are:

- Rue Montorgueil, 1st/Métro Les Halles
- Rue Mouffetard, 5th/Métro Censier-Daubenton
- Rue de Buci, 6th/Métro Mabillon
- Marché Raspail, 6th/Métro Rennes (open Sunday) (organic)
- Rue Cler, 7th/Métro École Militaire
- Marché Bastille on the boulevard Richard Lenoir, 11th/Métro Bastille (open Thursday and Sunday)
- Rue Daguerre, 14th/Métro Denfert-Rochereau
- Rue Poncelet, 17th/Métro Ternes
- Marché Jourdan along Boulevard Jourdan, 14th/Métro Porte d'Orléans (Wednesday and Saturday morning).

There are other places around Paris where you can also see and experience food in a unique setting. The area around the **Place de la Madeleine** (8th/Métro Madeleine) is packed with fabulous specialty food shops (the windows of the food store Fauchon are worth a trip by themselves), wine dealers, restaurants, and tea rooms. This is a perfect place to eat and purchase culinary souvenirs. There is something for every taste – but this is an upscale area, and can be expensive.

There are several areas in Paris where many restaurants are concentrated in small pockets. These are areas that are charming just in and of themselves, nice to walk through and nice to eat in, particularly outside on a nice evening.

One area is on **rue Pot-de-Fer** between la rue Tournefort and la rue Mouffetard, just off the market. It's a slip of a street but it's lined with charming restaurants with clothed tables set for dinner, colored lights hanging from the roof overhangs, and a uniquely Parisian ambiance (Métro Monge).

Uniquely Parisian is not the **Passage Brady** in the 10th arrondissement. Enter the narrow passage around 33 boulevard Strasbourg and find mostly Indian, but also Turkish and Moroccan, restaurants in an interestingly Indian setting. These are inexpensive restaurants in a working-class neighborhood, and the passage, while exotic in many ways, is not upscale (Métro Château d'Eau).

There are several restaurants and bars on the lovely **Place Sainte-Catherine** (enter from rue Caron off of rue St-Antoine) in the Marais. The Place Sainte-Catherine is a special, quiet respite in this fashionable area (Métro St-Paul). Highly recommended!

You'll find loads of restaurants **off of la rue Saint-Jacques** in the area around la rue Saint-Séverin and la rue de la Huchette in the 5th. This area, a short walk from Notre Dame, is filled with French, Italian, Greek and other restaurants jammed into small streets. It's a very pleasant walk, and you're bound to find somewhere to eat. Nearby in the 6th is the **cour du Commerce**, a tiny alleyway off of la rue St-André-des-Arts, which is lined with restaurants to fit all pocketbooks (Métros Saint-Michel, Odéon or Cluny-La Sorbonne).

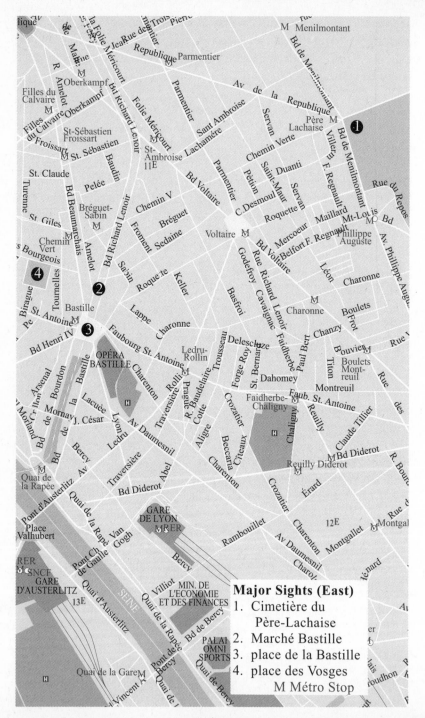

Major Sights (East)
1. Cimetière du Père-Lachaise
2. Marché Bastille
3. place de la Bastille
4. place des Vosges
   M Métro Stop

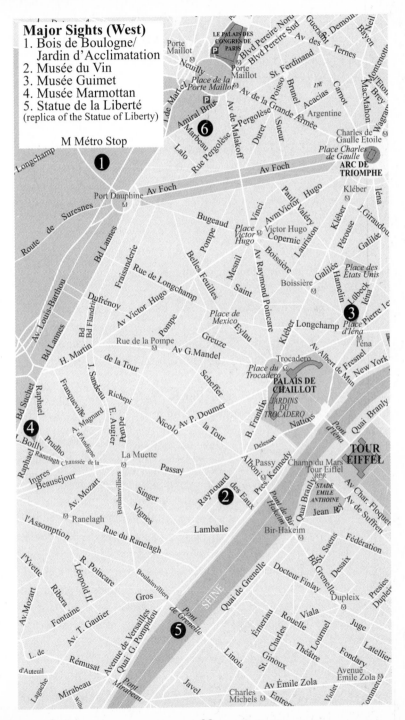

Major Sights (West)
1. Bois de Boulogne/
   Jardin d'Acclimatation
2. Musée du Vin
3. Musée Guimet
4. Musée Marmottan
5. Statue de la Liberté
(replica of the Statue of Liberty)

M Métro Stop

TEN SIMPLE RULES OF DINING IN PARIS

1. Avoid eating in a restaurant that has a menu written in English. We're against them for a number of reasons. One good reason is that at one restaurant, we were automatically given the English menu and we discovered as we walked out that it bore no relationship to the French menu which was more than twice as long.

2. Don't be afraid. They can't and won't hurt you. They are not laughing at you, they don't dislike you, they aren't even thinking about you. Waiters in France are trained professionals whose job is to serve you. Despite what you've heard, they want you to have a good time. Sometimes they are just mystified by what we do.

3. Don't ever call the waiter "garçon." Though sometimes in bars a Parisian will use this word, travelers should never use it.

4. Try to make reservations. This isn't as difficult as it seems; the words are similar in both languages and they'll get the gist of what you're trying to do. We often do a walk-by in the afternoon and stop in to make the reservation. When we go back that night they are almost always happy to see us again.

5. Return to a restaurant if you like it. If you have the luxury of time and can withstand the temptation to try other restaurants, you will always be treated better if they recognize you. Few travelers return to the same restaurant.

6. Parisians dine leisurely. Don't expect to get the same speed of service as at home. For the French, dinner is nearly a ritual. In its full-blown form, it begins with an *apéritif*. This is often accompanied by an *amuse-gueule*, a little snack of some sort. After this, you order an *hors-d'oeuvre*. Then comes an *entrée*, which is a first course – pâté or a composed salad, such as a salad with shrimp or hard-boiled eggs – and then the main course (*plat*) which will most likely be meat or fish. The main course is sometimes accompanied by or followed by a salad, but it is a simple green salad. After this, just when you think you're going to explode and have secretly unbuckled your belt, the *serveur* arrives with selections from the cheese platter that are followed by dessert, and, finally, coffee. But if you do not want to follow the French protocol, don't. Even if the waiter seems to disapprove, do what you like.

7. Don't talk loudly. You will notice that the French speak softly, Americans don't; we just can't help it. But believe us: Those loud voices coupled with running shoes, backpacks, "fanny packs," large, conspicuous guide books and cameras are like wearing a neon sign announcing that you are a tourist, an American tourist.

8. Stand your ground without being aggressive. In the years we've been traveling, it seems that waiters have become more relaxed about the rituals of eating, and will accommodate you if you insist on what you want – within reason, of course.

9. Visit a street vendor at least once in Paris. Whether it's sandwiches, hot dogs or crêpes, Parisian street vendors sell delicious "food on the run." Do yourself a favor, and sample some.

PARLEZ-VOUS?

Do you speak English?, parlez-vous anglais? (par lay voo ahn glay)

I don't speak French, je ne parle pas français (zhe ne parl pah frahn say)

I don't understand, je ne comprends pas (zhe ne kohm prahn pas)

I'd like a table, je voudrais une table (zhe voo dray ewn tabl)

I'd like to reserve a table, je voudrais réserver une table (zhe voo dray rayzehrvay ewn tabl)

waiter/sir, monsieur (muh-syuh) (never garçon!)

waitress/miss, mademoiselle (mad mwa zel)

menu, la carte (la cart) (not menu!)

wine list, la carte des vins (la cart day van)

no smoking, défense de fumer (day fahns de fu may)

10. Always be courteous. Remember that you are a guest in their country. There are simple things that the French do that we don't, like excusing yourself or saying please all the time. *S'il vous plaît* (seel voo play) after nearly everything is a safe way to be very polite. Seriously. A polite Parisian ALWAYS finishes a greeting (such as *bonjour* – hello) or affirmation (such as *oui* – yes) with a title. Thus, bonjour is always *bonjour, madame* or *bonjour, m'sieur* and yes or no is always *oui, m'sieur* or *oui, madame*. And just so you know, you say *bonjour*, which is essentially **hello**, all day and night.

Bon soir – **good evening** – is reserved for leaving and after 7:00 p.m., and *bonne nuit* – **good night** – is only used when you are actually on your way to bed.

3. FRENCH WINES

AN INTRODUCTION TO FRENCH WINE REGIONS
by Christine Humphrey, Founder and Editor of Grapegazette.com

One of the many wonderful things about visiting Paris is the availability of affordable French wines. Restaurants, wine bars, wine boutiques, and neighborhood markets are full of exciting wines not readily available in the U.S., Canada, and the U.K., if at all. Paris is full of opportunities to taste and enjoy these lesser-known wines.

When you think of French wines, Bordeaux, Burgundy, Champagne, and Châteauneuf-du-Pape come to mind. Wines from these regions have the reputation of being expensive, although some reasonable ones can be found in the U.S. Wines from these regions are the most widely accessible in the U.S. and therefore the best-known.

In Paris, while expensive wines will be on wine lists, the average French consumer will gravitate to the wonderful wines of France's many other regions, where a nice glass of wine can be had for €3,00-6,00 (or $5-8) per glass, and under €30,00 (or $40) per bottle. Also readily available are carafes or pichets of wine, for when you want a few glasses but not a whole bottle of wine. The "wines by the glass" offerings in most wine bars and bistros will feature wines from regions other than Bordeaux, Burgundy and Champagne. The "house wine" is even more reasonable and is often quite good.

The French place great emphasis on the concept of *terroir*, a "sense of place." They are proud of each region's local

France
FRENCH WINE REGIONS

cuisine and wine. In order to preserve and differentiate each region, there are many regulations in place that dictate what grapes can be grown where to best reflect the geology and climate of each region or *terroir*.

What is confusing about French wines is the label and trying to understand exactly what is in the bottle. In this hemisphere, the grape varietal, like Chardonnay, Cabernet Sauvignon, Pinot Noir, etc., is on the label. But in France, the region and producer take prominence, with no mention of the grape varietal with very few exceptions. So, when you see on a wine list, for example, "Corbieres" or "Chinon," you won't know what kind of wine you're getting. The locations are the **AOCs**, or in the most recent terminology, the **AOPs**, which are the specific **appellations or sub-regions** where the grapes are grown. While a good bartender, server, and certainly a sommelier can explain the French wines to you, it's nice to have an idea what to expect.

To understand what the label means, it is helpful to know what grapes grow in each region. What follows is a short guide to help you understand the major French wine regions.

ALSACE

This region is on the German border, near Strasbourg, and therefore a cooler wine region. The predominant wines are white, with some crémant or sparkling wines. **Riesling** and **Gewurztraminer** are the most prominent varietals, with **Pinot Gris**, **Pinot Blanc**, **Sylvaner**, and **Muscat** some other examples. These wines can be dry to sweet. Some Rieslings have a petrol aroma, while Gewurztraminer is quite floral. These wines are especially good with spicy foods.

BEAUJOLAIS

This region lies just north of Lyon and south of Burgundy. Gamay is the prominent grape and it produces a light, fruity red wine. While **Beaujolais Nouveau**, the "drink now" wine released the third week of every November, is the most widely recognized wine from this region, very nice reds from the **Brouilly**, **Fleurie**, **Morgon**, and **Moulin-a-Vent** AOCs (appellations) are quite nice and a less expensive alternative to some Burgundies.

BORDEAUX

This region, on the southern Atlantic coast of France, is world-famous for reds, and is divided into the left bank, Cabernet Sauvignon-dominant wines; and the right bank, Merlot-dominant wines. Some of the most famous and expensive wines come from the AOC/AOP appellations of **Pomerol**, **Pauillac**, **Saint-Emilion**, **Graves**, **Margaux**, and **Pessac-Leognan**. But excellent, more affordable Bordeaux wines come from **Bordeaux Superieur**, **Côte de Castillon**, **Cru Bourgeois**, **Entre-Deux-Mers**, **Médoc**, and **Haut-Médoc**. Additionally, Bordeaux produces world-class whites produced from Sémillon and Sauvignon Blanc grapes in both dry wines from some of the sub-regions previously mentioned, and beautiful sweet wines from Sauternes and Barsac.

BURGUNDY

A very complex region, with some of the most famous and expensive wines in the world. Think **Romanée-Conti**, **Richebourg**, **Corton-Charlemagne**, and **La Táche**. But there are more affordable wines from Burgundy that are not Grand Cru or Premier Cru that are quite lovely expressions of their *terroirs.* These are the Villages level and Bourgogne regional wines from various communes throughout Burgundy. Pinot Noir is "the" red grape and Chardonnay is "the" white grape. **Chablis** is a sub-region to the north that produces some nice, affordable whites, while reasonably priced wines can also be found in **Côte Chalonnaise** and the **Mâcon** to the south. Burgundy is a few hours southeast of Paris, with Beaune at its center, and some other communes that include **Nuits-Saint-Georges**, **Pommard** and **Morey-Saint-Denis**, to name a few. There are also sparkling crémant wines produced throughout the region.

CHAMPAGNE

This world-famous sparkling-wine region is the closet to Paris, located to the east. With just a very few exceptions, all sparkling wines called Champagne must be from this region. The grapes grown here are Pinot Noir, Chardonnay, and Pinot Meunier. Most are non-vintage, which means the grapes used are from various vintages. Vintage champagne is more expensive as it is less-produced than non-vintage. Towns in this region include **Épernay**, **Reims** (pronounced "Ronce") and **Troyes** (pronounced "Twa"). There are many day trips available from Paris to the region by train, coach, or minivan.

Coupe de Champagne.

CORSICA

Corse in French, this region is on the island in the Mediterranean, north of Italy's Sardinia. These wines are gaining in popularity, with the names of **Ajaccio** (the prinicipal city), **Corse**, and **Vin de Corse** on the labels. Wines can be dry or sweet; red, white, or rosé; medium- to full-bodied; and produced from warm-weather grape varietals such as Rolle (Vermentino), Ugni Blanc, Grenache, Cinsault, Carignan, Muscat, and Aleatico which are also found along the Mediterranean coast.

JURA

The wines from this region, adjacent to Switzerland, are produced from cool-weather red and white varietals that include Savagnin, Pinot Noir, Poulsard, Trousseau, and Chardonnay. They can be dry, sparkling, or sweet; and are light- to medium-body. Some are made into rosés for summer enjoyment.

WINE TERMS

vin, wine
vin blanc, white wine
vin rouge, red wine
vin chambré, wine served at room temperature
vin cuit, sweet dessert wine
vin de maison, house wine
vin de pays, wine guaranteed to originate in a certain region (country wine)
vin de table, table wine
vin de xérès, sherry
vin doux, sweet wine/dessert wine
vin doux naturel, naturally sweet wine

Sub-regions include **Arbois**, **Côtes du Jura**, **Crémant de Jura**, and **L'Étoile**. Nearby cities are Arbois, Besancon, and Geneva (Switzerland).

LANGUEDOC-ROUSSILLON

The southernmost wine region on the mainland of France, it is the country's largest wine region in both surface and production. Its geography extends from just west of the Rhôné, near Nîmes, to the Spanish border at Banyuls. Winemaking in this region dates back to Roman times. The wines are light to full-bodied; white, red, and rosé; dry; sparkling (**Crémant de Limoux**, **Blanquette de Limoux**); sweet; and fortified (**Vins du Naturel**). The predominant grapes are Grenache, Syrah, Mourvedre, Carignan, Cinsault, Cabernet Sauvignon, Merlot, Cabernet Franc, Picpoul, Bourboulenc, Mauzac, Marsanne, Rousanne, Chenin Blanc, Maccabeo, Rolle, Viognier, and Muscat Blanc à Petits Grains. Some of the prominent sub-regions are **Banyuls**, **Corbieres**, **Côteaux du Languedoc**, **Côtes du Roussillon**, **Fitou**, **Limoux**, **Maury**, **Minervois**, **Rivesaltes**, and **Saint-Chinian**. It's a beautiful and diverse region that includes the cities of Montpellier, Narbonne, Carcassonne, Perpignan, Banyuls, and Limoux; and includes mountains and the sea that influence the region's climate. This region's wines are very popular in wine bars and restaurants, and represent great value and nice quality, especially of late.

LOIRE

This beautiful region, comprised of troglodyte caves and châteaux, is the garden of France. It extends from the east in Sancerre to Nantes by the Atlantic. The shallow Loire River runs through it. Cabernet Franc, Chenin Blanc, and Sauvignon Blanc are the grapes here. Dry, sparkling, sweet, and white wines are produced. These wines, like those of Languedoc-Roussillon, are featured throughout wine bars and restaurants, are affordable, and of excellent quality. Some of the prominent sub-regions are **Anjou, Bourgeuil, Chinon, Sancerre, Saumur, Touraine** and **Vouvray.** Towns include Tours, Angers, Chinon, Saumur, and Nantes.

PROVENCE

This region is to the east of the Rhône, from south of Avignon to the Mediterranean. It produces rosés, reds, and whites made from basically the same grapes as in the neighboring Languedoc-Roussillon. Prominent sub-regions include **Côtes de Provence, Bandol, Cassis,** and **Les Baux-de-Provence.** Cities include Aix-en-Provence, Arles, Cassis, St Remy, Nice, and the adjacent, major port of Marseilles.

> **MORE WINE TERMS**
> *vin du pays,* country wine
> *vin gris,* pink wine
> *vin liquoreux,* sweet wine
> *vin mousseux,* sparkling wine
> *vin nouveau,* new wine
> *vin ordinaire,* table wine
> *vin rosé,* rosé wine
> *vin sec,* dry wine

RHÔNE

This region is actually divided into two distinct geographical areas: the Northern Rhône, just south of Lyon; and the Southern Rhône near Avignon, including Châteauneuf-du-Pape. In the north, the climate is more continental, influenced by the northerly *mistral* winds, and Syrah is king. (The mistral wind blows 30 to 60 miles per hour, about 100 days of the year. It begins above the Alps and Massif Central Mountains, gaining speed as it heads south.) Viognier, its white counterpart, is also grown, and often added to the wines of Côte-Rotie; but stands on its own in Condrieu. The wines are medium- to full-bodied. Other prominent sub-regions include **Cornas, Crozes-Hermitages, Hermitage,** and **Saint-Joseph.** These wines can be quite expensive but are some of the most elegant wines in France, especially when aged. But there are affordable ones as well. In the Southern Rhône the climate is Mediterranean, also influenced by the *mistral,* and is home to the Rhône varietals of Grenache, Syrah, Mourvedre, Cinsault, Counoise, Carigan, Viognier, Marsanne, Rousanne, Bourbelenc, Picpoul, and Clairette. The wines produced are more full-bodied and include the famous **Châteauneuf-du-Pape, Côtes du Rhône, Costières de Nîmes, Gigondas, Lirac, Rasteau, Tavel** (exclusively rosé), and **Vacqueyras.** Other cities in the Southern Rhône include Orange, Nîmes, and Carpentras.

SAVOIE (SAVOY)

This small, beautiful region is adjacent to Jura, the Alps, and Switzerland. The wines are dry, light- to medium-bodied, and include the sub-regions of **Bugey**, **Crépy** and **Vin de Savoie**. Varietals grown here are red and white colder-climate grapes, including Mondeuse, Jacquere, Roussette, Chardonnay, Gamay, and Pinot Noir. Cities include Annecy and Geneva.

SOUTH WEST FRANCE (SUD OUEST)

This region is, appropriately, in the southwestern corner of France, from south of the Bordeaux region to the Spanish border, in Basque country.

Wines here are full-bodied and tannic, with the predominant grapes being Tannat, Cot (Malbec), Merlot, Cabernet Sauvignon, Jurançon, Duras, Fer, Gros Manseng, Petit Manseng, Muscadelle, Ugni Blanc, and Sauvignon Blanc. Dry, sparkling, and sweet wines are produced. Sub-regions include **Bergerac**, **Cahors**, **Gaillac**, **Jurançon** and **Madiran**. Cities include Bergerac, Cahors, Gaillac, and nearby Toulouse.

ORGANIC, BIODYNAMIC & "NATURAL" WINES

Organic and biodynamic wines are gaining in popularity worldwide, and especially in France. Many Parisian restaurants and wine bars, including Le Verre Volé and Les Papilles (both found in this book), serve them.

Organic wine is made with organically grown grapes, without chemical pesticides, fertilizers, herbicides, or fungicides.

Biodynamic wines utilize biodynamic-farming practices, advocated by Austrian scientist and philosopher Rudolph Steiner in 1924, well before today's organic movement. Based on spiritual, ecological, and mystical principles, biodynamic farming is a self-contained ecosystem of animals, insects, birds, and plants that promotes healthy soils and crops.

You may also come across natural wine – "vin naturel." Because there is still no clear definition of the term within the wine industry, nor are these "natural" wines recognized or regulated yet as a wine category in the European Union, the term remains controversial.

4. RESTAURANTS, WINE BARS & WINE SHOPS

1ST ARRONDISSEMENT
Louvre/Les Halles

The 1st is the center of Paris where many tourist attractions are found, including the Louvre, Palais Royal and Jardin des Tuileries.

SIGHTS
Musée National du Louvre

The Louvre is the world's greatest art museum. The buildings that house the museum were constructed in the 13th century as a fortress. Today, the inner courtyard is the site of the fantastic glass pyramid, designed by the famous architect I.M. Pei, that serves as the main entrance to the museum.

The Louvre is the largest art museum in the world, the largest building in Paris, and it's in the largest palace in Europe. It's home to famous works like the Vénus de Milo and Mona Lisa. Adjoining the museum is the Jardin des Tuileries. You'll enjoy bubbling fountains, statues, flowers and trees. Sit down and relax in this beautiful garden in the middle of Paris. Nearby is

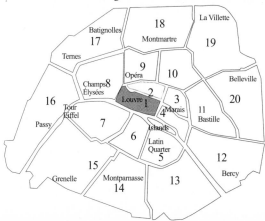

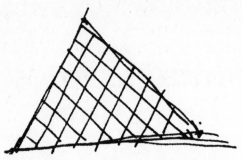

Palais Royal. You come here to take a break in the calm, beautiful garden. For more information on the garden, see later in this Chapter. *Info: 1ˢᵗ/Métro Palais-Royal. 34-36 quai du Louvre. Tel. 01/40.20.53.17. Open Mon, Thu, Sat-Sun 9am-6pm; Wed and Fri 9am-9:45pm. Closed Tue. Closed Jan 1, May1 and Dec 25. Admission: €11. Under 18 free and free the first Sunday of the month and July 14. Under 26 free after 6pm on Fri. €12 for exhibitions in Napoléon Hall. Combined permanent collection and temporary exhibits €15. www.louvre.fr.*

Musée de l'Orangerie

The "Orangerie" is located in a former 19th-century greenhouse and is situated at the west end of the Tuileries garden. It's home to a collection of paintings from the late 19th century and the first half of the 20th century (including 15 Cézannes, 24 Renoirs, 10 Matisses and 12 Picassos). Of particular note are the large Water Lilies by Monet. The Orangerie is small and manageable. It's magnificent. *Info: 1ˢᵗ/Métro Concorde. 1 place de la Concorde. Tel. 01/44.77.80.07. Open Wed-Mon 9am-6pm. Closed Tue. Admission: €7.50, under 18 free. Free on the first Sun of each month. English tours Mon and Thu at 2:30pm. www.musee-orangerie.fr.*

Ste-Chapelle

On a sunny day, you'll be dazzled by nearly 6,600 square feet of stained glass at this Gothic masterpiece. Fifteen windows depict biblical scenes from the Garden of Eden to the Apocalypse (the large rose window). Built in 1246, it took less than two years to build, an amazing feat when one realizes that Notre-Dame took over two centuries to complete. *Info: 1ˢᵗ/Métro Cité. 4 boulevard du Palais. Tel. 01/53.40.60.80. Open daily Mar-Oct 9:30am-6pm, Nov-Feb 9am-5pm. Closed Jan 1, May 1 and Dec 25. Admission: €8.50 adults, €5.50 ages 18-25, under 18 free. Combined admission for Conciergerie is €12.50. sainte-chapelle.monuments-nationaux.fr/en/.*

You can visit the **Musée de la Conciergerie**, especially if you're a history buff. It's on the same street as Ste-Chapelle. The Conciergerie is a 14th-century prison where over 2,600 people waited to have their heads chopped off, including Marie-Antoinette, during the French Revolution's Reign of Terror. It's a grim but interesting museum. *Info: 1ˢᵗ/Métro Cité. 2 boulevard du Palais. Tel. 01/53.40.60.80. Open daily 9:30am-6pm. Closed Jan 1, May 1, Dec 25. Admission: €8.50 adults, €5.50 ages 18-25, under 18 free. Combined admission with Ste-Chapelle is €12.50. conciergerie.monuments-nationaux.fr.*

If you're interested in photography, you can visit the **Galerie Nationale du Jeu de Paume** in the northeast corner of the Jardin des Tuileries. Named after a ball game similar to tennis that was played here, this museum houses the national video and photography museum. *Info: 1ˢᵗ/Métro Concorde. Northeast corner of the Jardin des Tuileries at 1 place de la Concorde. Tel. 01/47.03.12.50. Open Tue 11am-9pm, Wed-Sun 11am-7pm. Closed Mon. Admission: €8.50, under 10 free. www.jeudepaume.org.*

You can also head to the **gardens of the Palais Royal**. Built in 1632, it now houses ministries of the French government (so you won't be able to look inside). You come here to take a break in the calm, beautiful garden. The buildings around the garden, built in the 1700s, are home to everything from stamp shops to art galleries. If you're interested in sculpture, check out the 280 controversial (meaning some did not like them) prison-striped columns by Daniel Buren that were placed in the main courtyard. Very 80s! There are plenty of comfortable cafés here to have a nightcap. *Info: 1st/Métro Palais-Royal. place Palais Royal (across the rue de Rivoli from the Louvre).*

RESTAURANTS & WINE BARS
O Château
"Coming to Paris and not tasting good French wines is like going to the U.S. and not trying a good burger," says Olivier Magny of O Château. This energetic French *sommelier* will guide you through a fun, informative and relaxing wine tasting. They now have opened the largest wine bar in Paris. *Info: 1st/Métro Louvre-Rivoli. 68 rue Jean-Jacques Rousseau. Tel. 01/44.73.97.80. www.o-chateau.com (reservations). Admission: from €30 per person.*

Juvenile's
This inexpensive, unpretentious wine bar serves light meals and has a large, interesting New- and Old-World wine selection. Friendly and fun. Order traditional wine-bar fare or, if you're tired of French food, try the haggis. (The owner, originally from Scotland, has just turned over the place to his

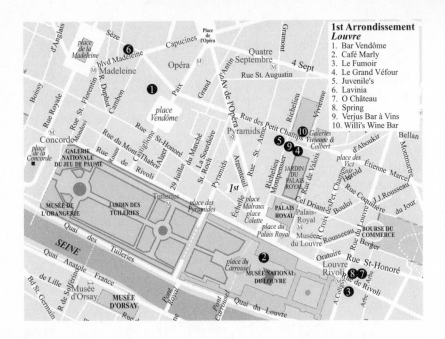

daughter.) *Info: 1st/Métro Bourse. 47 rue de Richelieu (near rue des Petits Champs). Tel. 01/42.97.46.49. Closed Sun and Mon (lunch). Inexpensive-Moderate.*

Willi's Wine Bar

British owners serving specialties with Mediterranean influences. A great wine list, and a favorite of many travelers to Paris. Try the *veau fermier* (free-range veal) in a citrus and ginger sauce. *Info: 1st/Métro Bourse. 13 rue des Petits-Champs (near rue Vivienne). Tel. 01/42.61.05.09 . Closed Sun and part of Aug. www.williswinebar.com. Moderate.*

Verjus Bar à Vins

A French wine bar with an American twist. Braden Perkins, an American chef and owner of the restaurant Verjus, opened this popular eatery. Small plates (there are usually three choices) and an excellent wine selection from Laura Adrian, the *sommelier*. Try the delicious fried chicken sandwich! No reservations. *Info: 1st/Métro Bourse, Pyramides or. Palais-Royal. 47 rue de Montpensier. Tel. 01/42.97.54.40. Lunch Tue-Fri, dinner Mon-Fri. Closed Sat and Sun. Moderate.*

Le Fumoir

This bar and restaurant is located near the Louvre. It's known for its Sunday brunch, salads, happy hour and *gâteau chocolat* (chocolate cake). There's a library in the back where you can have a drink and read (and exchange your own books for the ones in their library). *Info: 1st/Métro Louvre-Rivoli. 6 rue de l'Amiral-de Coligny (between rue de Rivoli and the River Seine). Tel. 01/42.92.00.24. Open daily 11am to 2am. Closed part of Aug. www.lefumoir. com. Inexpensive-Moderate.*

Le Grand Véfour *Historic Restaurant*

This famous restaurant, in the arcades of the Palais-Royal, opened in 1784; and features early nineteenth-century décor of large mirrors in gilded frames. Guy Martin, a Michelin-starred chef, oversees your dining experience. Extensive wine selection. *Info: 1st/Métro Palais-Royal. 17 rue de Beaujolais. Tel. 01/42.96.56.27. www.grand-vefour.com. Closed Sat and Sun. Very Expensive.*

Spring

Who would have thought that a Chicago-born chef would be creating a buzz in Paris dining? Daniel Rose has moved from his tiny restaurant into a modern, sleek space near the Louvre. Reserve well in advance. The menu changes daily and you'll be served what everyone else is having. A delicious experience that you won't soon forget. Interesting wine list. *Info: 1st/Métro Louvre-Rivoli. 6 rue Bailleul (one block north of rue de Rivoli, off of rue du Louvre). Tel. 01/45.96.05.72. Open dinner Tue-Sat. Reservations required. www.springparis.fr. Very Expensive.*

Lavinia

The largest wine shop in Paris with 2000 foreign wines, 3000 French wines and 1000 spirits, priced from €3 to €600. Drink any bottle from the shop at the wine bar. Lunch served with wine, of course. *Info: 1st/Métro Madeleine. 3-5 boulevard de la Madeleine. Tel. 01/42.97.20.27. Open Mon-Sat 10am-8pm.*

DRINKING

Bar Vendôme

A choice for an *apéritif* (before-dinner drink) or *digestif* (after-dinner drink) is this bar at the swanky Hôtel Ritz. Dress up and expect to hand out quite a few euros for your drinks (cocktails cost at least €30). There's also a selection of wine by the glass. _Info_: *1st/Métro Opéra. 15 place Vendôme. Tel. 01/43.16.30.30. Open daily 10:30am-2am. The bar and Hôtel Ritz will reopen in summer 2014 after restoration.*

CAFÉ MARLY

This café overlooks the pyramid at the Louvre and no place in Paris has a better setting. Standard bistro fare served by waiters in suits. It is a great place for a relaxing lunch or you can come here after dinner and end your day with a glass of champagne. Definitely worth the cost! *Info: 1st/Métro Musée du Louvre/ Palais-Royal. 93 rue de Rivoli. Tel. 01/49.26.06.60. Open daily 8am to 2am.*

2ⁿᵈ ARRONDISSEMENT
La Bourse

The 2nd is primarily a business district, but it has a few sights worth noting.

SIGHTS

The **Eglise St-Eustache** is a beautiful Gothic and Renaissance church dating back to 1532. Rembrandt's *Pilgrimage to Emmaus* is here. The church hosts contemporary art exhibits and organ concerts featuring the ornate and immense pipe organ. The organ itself is new (1989), but is housed in a 19th-century carved casing. It was designed with the console at ground level so that the audience can see the organist playing. The free concerts are held most Sunday evenings. *Info: 2nd/Métro Les Halles. 2 rue du Jour. Admission: Free.*

The French stock exchange (**Bourse**) is a lot more sedate than Wall Street, and you'll need your passport to get in. Tours are only in French. Headsets are available with English-commentary. The stock exchange is housed in an 1800s Romanesque temple. How French! *Info: 2nd/Métro Bourse. 4 place de la Bourse. Tel. 01/49.27.55.52. Open weekday afternoons.*

In the 1800s, there were 137 **glass-roofed shopping arcades** (*passages*) in Paris. Only 24 remain. The oldest, dating back to 1800, is **Passage des Panoramas**, *11 blvd. Montmartre* (known for its stamps). Nearby are **Passage**

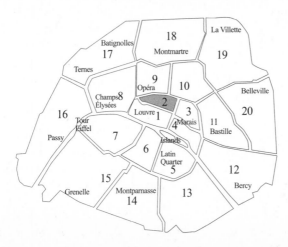

Verdeau, *4-6 rue de la Grange Batelière* and **Passage Jouffroy**, *12 blvd. Montmartre. Passages* are luminous and practical. The glass roofs not only admit light, but they shelter shoppers from rain. *2nd/Métro Grands Boulevards.*

Several of the wine bars listed below are located in *passages*. Our favorite one is **Passage du Grand Cerf** in the Montorgueil area. It's home to 33 fashionable shops and a restaurant (**Le Pas Sage**). Don't miss **Rickshaw** at number 7. You'll find unusual gifts from throughout the world. *Info: 2nd/ Métro Etienne Marcel. 145 rue Saint-Denis/rue Marie Stuart. Open Mon-Sat 8:30am-8pm.*

RESTAURANTS & WINE BARS

Aux Lyonnais *Historic Restaurant*
This beautiful century-old bistro has been renovated and serves the cuisine of Lyon. Try the *sanglier* (wild boar) when available. The wine of choice is Beaujolais. It's part of the Alain Ducasse group. *Info: 2nd/ Métro Bourse. 32 rue Saint-Marc (off of rue de Richelieu). Tel. 01/42.96.65.04. Closed Sat (lunch), Sun and Mon. www. auxlyonnais.com. Expensive.*

2nd Arrondissement *Bourse*
1. L'Art Source
2. Aux Lyonnais
3. Coinstot Vino/Noglu/
   Passages
4. Frenchie
5. Le Grand Colbert/Legrand Filles et Fils
6. L'Hédoniste
7. Osteria Ruggera

Le Grand Colbert
Historic Restaurant
Housed in a restored historic building, serving traditional brasserie cuisine. Known for its seafood tray. This stunning restaurant was featured in the movie *Something's Gotta Give*, so lots of tourists. *Info: 2nd/ Métro Bourse. 2 rue Vivienne (near the Place des Victoires). Tel. 01/42.86.87.88. Closed part of Aug. www.legrandcolbert.com. Moderate-Expensive.*

L'Hédoniste

This unassuming, typical Parisian bistro near Les Halles will not disappoint. You can dine in the small, storefront dining room with stone walls or outside in good weather. Several choices stand out: the delicious *merlu* (hake fish) or *agneau figahelli, jus olive* (lamb with pasta and an olive sauce). Try one of the bottles of wine from the Luberon region. *Info: 2nd/Métro Sentier or Les Halles. 14 rue Léopold-Bellan (off rue Montmartre). Tel. 01/40.26.87.33. Closed Sat (lunch), Sun and Mon. www.lhedoniste.com. Moderate - Expensive.*

Osteria Ruggera

This intimate restaurant in the increasingly hip, pedestrian Montorgueil area serves delicious Italian dishes. Try the *dégustation de 5 entrées pour 2 personnes* (five antipasti for two persons) and wash it down with a bottle of Primitivo. *Info: 2nd/Métro Etienne Marcel. 35 rue Tiquetonne (off of rue Montorgueil). Tel. 01/40.26.13.91. Open daily. No lunch Sat and Sun. www.osteria-ruggera.com. Moderate.*

Frenchie Bar à Vins

You can sample Chef Gregory Marchand's dishes at this wine-bar annex to his (famously difficult to get into) bistro Frenchie. The menu consists of small plates. Try *terrine de campagne* and down it with a glass of wine from the interesting wine list. To score a table, you must arrive before 7:00 p.m. *Info: 2nd/Métro Sentier. 6 rue du Nil (between rue d'Aboukir and rue Réaumur). No telephone. No reservations. No lunch. Closed Sat and Sun. www.frenchie-restaurant. com. Moderate. Restaurant Frenchie is at 5 rue du Nil, Tel. 01/40.39.96.19 (reservations). Closed Sat and Sun. Expensive.*

Down the street at 9 rue du Nil is **Frenchie To Go** featuring fish and chips, pickles, smoked bacon, and a delicious reuben sandwich. No reservations. There are 15 seats if you want to eat on the premises, and you can wash down your food with ginger beer. *Info: Open Tue-Sat 8am-6pm. Lunch served noon-4pm. Breakfast served all day. Inexpensive-Moderate.*

Legrand Filles et Fils

In the elegant Galerie Vivienne, this wine shop and bar has been run by the Legrand family for over three generations. Check out the cork-covered ceiling. Sandwiches, salads and cheese platters. A great place for a light lunch. *Info: 2nd/Métro Bourse. 1 rue de la Bourse. Tel. 01/42.60.07.12. Open Mon-Sat 10am-7pm. Closed Sun. www.caves-legrand.com. Moderate-Expensive.*

Coinstot Vino

Guillaume Dupré runs this casual wine bar located in the passage des Panoramas. In addition to the superior wine list, you can order small plates (such as wild bass on endive) or select from a few main courses. *Info: 2nd/ Métro Grands Boulevards. 26 passage des Panoramas. Tel. 01/44.82.08.54. Closed Sunday. www.coinstot-vino.com. Moderate.*

L'Art Source

This attractive wine bar with stone walls and beamed ceiling is located on a pedestrian street off of rue Montorgueil. The helpful English-speaking staff will guide you through the wines by the glass. Small plates offered include mini-burgers and ceviche. In warm weather, there's a small and comfortable area in front where you can sit outside. Great choice for a late-night drink and snack. *Info: 2nd/Métro Etienne Marcel. 6 rue Marie Stuart (off of rue Montorgueil). Tel. 09/82.55.00.49. Open Tue-Sat 6:30pm to 2am. www.lartsource.com. Inexpensive-Moderate.*

MARKETS

Rue Montorgueil in the location of one of the best fish and meat markets in the city. You'll also find wine shops and bistros along this pedestrian street. The renowned **Stohrer** is also here. The Parisian favorite of *baba au*

rhum (spongecake soaked in rum) was invented at this *pâtisserie*. When available, try a *macaron*. It isn't the sticky coconut version, but two almond-meringue cookies, flavored with vanilla, chocolate, coffee, pistachio, or other flavor, stuck together with butter cream. *Info: 2nd/ Métro Les Halles. 51 rue Montorgueil. Tel. 01/42.33.38.20. Open daily. Closed part of Aug.*

SHOPS
A. Simon
This kitchenware shop is where the chefs shop. You can fill your own kitchen with pans, wine glasses and other glassware, and some stuff you find only in bistros (like paper doilies and chalkboards). *Info: 2nd/Métro Les Halles. 48 rue Montmartre. Tel. 01/42.33.71.65. Open Tue-Sat 9am-6:30pm, Mon 1:30pm-6:30pm.*

ORGANIC RESTAURANT, FOOD SHOPS & MARKETS

Noglu is a gluten-free restaurant (and take-out) that also offers some lactose-free dishes. Excellent desserts. There is a decent selection of organic wines. *Info: 2nd/ Métro Bourse or Grands Boulevards. 16 Passage des Panoramas. Tel. 01/40.25.41.24. Closed Sun. www. noglu.fr. Moderate.*

Paris is embracing the organic-food movement. There are several grocery stores featuring organic products (*Closed Sun.*):

BioCoop, throughout Paris, including *44 bd. de Grenelle, 15th/Métro Bir-Hakeim or Dupleix, www. biocoop.fr.*

Naturalia, throughout Paris, including *36 rue Monge, 4th/Métro Monge, www.naturalia.fr.*

There are also several organic outdoor markets, including **Marché bio Raspail**, *boulevard Raspail, 6th/Métro Rennes (Sun.)*; **Marché bio Brancusi**, place *Brancusi, 14th/Métro Gaité (Sat.)*; and **Marché bio Batignolles**, *boulevard des Batignolles,17th/Métro Place de Clichy (Sat.).*

3ʳᵈ Arrondissement
Beaubourg/Marais

The Marais is comprised of roughly the 3rd and 4th arrondissements on the Right Bank. This area, with its small streets and beautiful squares, is filled with interesting shops. It's home to both a thriving Jewish community and a large gay community. It's considered the *cœur historique*, historic heart of Paris. Sights include the Musée Picasso.

SIGHTS

Musée Picasso
The Musée Picasso has the largest Picasso collection in the world (not to mention works by Renoir, Cézanne, Degas and Matisse). *Info: 3ʳᵈ/Métro St-Sébastien or St-Paul. 5 rue de Thorigny. Tel. 01/42.71.25.21. Reopening after years of renovation. www.musee-picasso.fr.*

Musée Carnavalet-Histoire de Paris
In the 1700s, the Hôtel Carnavalet was presided over by Madame de Sévigné who chronicled French society in hundreds of letters written to her daughter. We went kicking and screaming into this museum as it sounded so very boring. We were wrong. You'll find antiques, portraits, and artifacts dating back to the late 1700s. The section on the French Revolution with its guillotines is especially interesting, as is the royal bedroom. There are

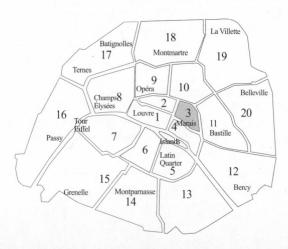

exhibits across the courtyard at the **Hôtel le Peletier de St-Fargeau**. Truly an interesting museum of the history of Paris. *Info: 3rd/Métro St-Paul. 23 rue de Sévigné. Tel. 01/44.59.58.58. Open Tue-Sun 10am-6pm. Closed Mon. Admission: Permanent collection is free. €7.50 for exhibits. www.carnavalet. paris.fr.*

The **Musée Cognacq-Jay**, located in the Hôtel Donon, an elegant mansion, houses the 18th-century art and furniture owned by Ernest Cognacq, the founder of La Samaritaine department store. Cognacq once bragged that he was not a lover of art and that he had never visited the Louvre. Perhaps it was his wife, Louise Jay, who had the sense to compile such an amazing art collection, including works by Rembrandt, Fragonard and Boucher. *Info: 3rd/Métro St-Paul. 8 rue Elzévir. Tel. 01/40.27.07.21. Open Tue-Sun 10am-6pm. Closed Mon. Admission: Free.*

Musée des Arts et Métiers

A huge interactive museum of science and industry. It's located in the former church of St-Martin des Champs. *Info: 3rd/Métro Arts et Métiers. 60 rue Réaumur. Tel. 01/53.01.82.00. Open Tue-Sun 10am-6pm (Thu until 9:30pm). Closed Mon. Admission: €6.50, under 18 free. www.arts-et-metiers.net.*

Musée de l'Histoire de France/Musée des Archives Nationales

This museum houses France's most famous documents, including some written by Joan of Arc, Marie-Antoinette and Napoléon. It's located in the Hôtel de Clisson, a palace dating back to 1371, the highlight of which is the incredibly ornate, oval-shaped Salon Ovale. *Info: 3rd/Métro Hôtel de Ville. 60 rue des Francs-Bourgeois. Tel. 01/40.27.60.96. Mon and Wed-Fri 10am-5:30pm, Sat-Sun 2pm-5:30pm. Closed Tue. Admission: €6, under 18 free.*

RESTAURANTS & WINE BARS

Au Bascou

This tiny bistro serves Basque specialties such as *piperade* (a spicy omelet). It doesn't look like much from the outside, but the food will not disappoint. Try the delicious *épaule d'agneau* (lamb shoulder) or *cabillaud poêlé* (fried cod). Interesting regional wine list. Too bad they're closed on weekends. *Info: 3rd/Métro Arts-et-Métiers. 38 rue Réaumur (at rue Volta). Tel. 01/42.72.69.25. Closed Sat, Sun and part of Aug. www.au-bascou.fr. Moderate.*

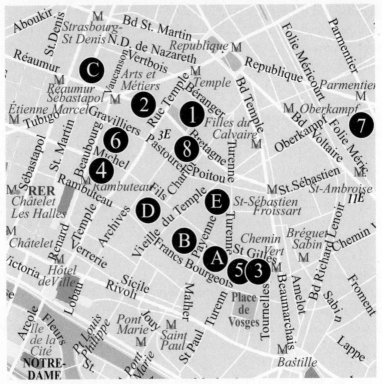

3rd Arrondissement *Beaubourg/Marais*

1. L'Aller Retour/Le Barav'
2. Au Bascou
3. Chez Janou
4. Le Hangar
5. Le Petit Marché
6. Le Taxi Jaune
7. Al Taglio
8. Versant Vins

A. Musée Carnavalet
B. Musée Cognacq-Jay
C. Musée Arts et Métiers
D. Musée de l'Histoire de France
E. Musée Picasso

Chez Janou

Everyone seems to be having a great time at this bistro, a few blocks from the place des Vosges. Provençal and straightforward French food (very good *entrecôte*). Decent-priced wines with an emphasis on those from Provence. Known for its selection of *pastis* (anise-flavored aperitif) and delicious bowl of *mousse au chocolat* (chocolate mousse). Not the greatest food in Paris, but certainly lots of fun. *Info: 3rd/Métro Chemin Vert. 2 rue Roger-Verlomme (at rue des Tournelles). Open daily. Tel. 01/42.72.28.41. www.chezjanou.com. Moderate.*

Le Taxi Jaune

You'll find the intimate "Yellow Taxi" on a backstreet in the Marais. The menu changes regularly and although it often includes offal and horse (*cheval*), there are plenty of other choices. Service is friendly, unobtrusive, and unhurried. Try the pumpkin and vegetable soup when available. If you're looking for a relaxing dining experience in the Marais, you've found the place. *Info:* 3rd/Métro Arts-et-Méiters. 13 rue Chapon (between rue du Temple and rue Beaubourg). Tel. 01/42.76.00.40. Closed Sat and Sun. Moderate.

Le Hangar

Nothing fancy about this bistro near the Pompidou Center. Classic French food at reasonable prices. Excellent *gâteau au chocolat*. *Info:* 3rd/Métro Rambuteau. 12 impasse Berthaud (off of rue Beaubourg). Tel. 01/42.74.55.44. Closed Sun., Mon. and Aug. No credit cards. Inexpensive-Moderate.

Le Barav'

This wine bar near the place de la République serves salads, sandwiches, cheese platters, and *charcuterie*. Try a delicious *tartine* (open-faced sandwich). You can select a wine by the glass (from €4-€7) or buy a bottle from the wine shop next door. *Info:* 3rd/Métro République. 6 rue Charles François Dupuis (off of rue Béranger). Tel. 01/48.04.57.59. Lunch Mon-Fri. Dinner Tue-Sat. Closed Sunday. www.lebarav.fr. Inexpensive-Moderate.

L'Aller Retour

Expect a leisurely meal at this modern bistro in the increasingly hip northern Marais (on the same street as Le Barav' above). Superb wine list and excellent meat dishes (try the *entrecôte*). Good burgers, too. *Info:* 3rd/Métro République. 5 rue Charles François Dupuis (off of rue Béranger). Tel. 01/42.78.01.21. Closed Sun and Mon. Moderate.

Le Petit Marché

This café/restaurant is located on a small street off the attractive place des Vosges. It's busy, noisy, and jam-packed (don't come here if you don't like to be seated in cramped quarters). Helpful and friendly staff. You'll find French cuisine with Asian influences such as fresh tuna tartar (*thon cru*) with toasted sesame seeds served with a Thai sauce. Excellent raspberry (*framboise*) dessert. Well worth a visit! *Info:* 3rd/Métro Chemin Vert. 9 rue Béarn. Tel. 01/42.72.06.07. Open daily. Moderate.

Versant Vins

This little wine bar is located in the Marché des Enfants Rouges, a covered market in the northern Marais. All the wines offered are organic. If you like any of the wines offered by the glass, you can purchase a bottle. They'll also recommend something to go with what you're taking home from the market. In the colder months, it's semi-sheltered and they also provide you with blankets. *Info: 3rd/Métro Filles du Calvaire. 39 Rue de Bretagne. Tel. 01/42/72.34.85. Closed Sun (evening) and Mon. www.versantvins.com Inexpensive-Moderate.*

Al Taglio

You'll find some of the best pizza in Paris at this inexpensive eatery. Try the margherita pizza (tomato, mozzarella and basil) and wash it down with some cheap wine by the carafe. *Info: 3rd/Métro Parmentier. 2 bis rue Neuve Popincourt (off of rue Oberkampf). Tel. 01/43.38.12.00. Open daily. Inexpensive.*

COOKING CLASS

Paule Caillat, who speaks fluent English, operates her unique business **Promenades Gourmandes** from her apartment. Groups of two to eight (mostly Americans) meet her at a café, visit a market to purchase ingredients for lunch, and then head to her apartment to cook a meal including a cheese tasting. It's a truly hands-on and mouth-full experience for food lovers. *Info: 3rd/ Métro Arts et Métiers. 38 rue Notre Dame de Nazareth. Tel. 01/48.04.56.84. Admission: Classes are held Tue-Fri. €270-290 for a half-day session. Gourmet walking tour without the class is €280 for a party of two or more. Reservations can be made through www. promenadesgourmandes.com.*

4ᵀᴴ ARRONDISSEMENT
Marais/Île St-Louis

The 4th Arrondissement is comprised of the Marais and the islands in the Seine River. Sights include the Cathédrale Notre-Dame, the Pompidou Center, and the lovely place des Vosges.

SIGHTS
Cathédrale Notre-Dame

Notre-Dame is one of the greatest achievements of Gothic architecture. It took nearly 200 years to complete the cathedral. It's so huge that it can accommodate over 6,000 visitors. The interior is dominated by three beautiful (and huge) rose windows, and has a 7,800-pipe organ. Inside along the walls are individual chapels dedicated to saints. The most famous chapel is that of Joan of Arc. The sacristy houses relics, manuscripts and religious garments. You can climb the 387 steps of the north tower for a grand view of Paris. You'll also have a great view of the cathedral's famous gargoyles. If you don't want to climb the tower, make sure you take a look at the sides of the church. You'll see the "flying buttresses" (50-foot beams that support the Gothic structure). *Info: 4th/Métro Cité. 6 place du Parvis Notre-Dame. Tel. 01/42.34.56.10 (cathedral). Tel. 01/53.10.07.00 (tower). Open daily 8am-6:45pm (until 7:15pm on Sat and Sun). Treasury open Mon-Fri 9:30am-6pm (until 6:30 on Sat), Sun 1:30pm-6:30pm). Tower open daily Apr-Sep 10am-6:30pm (until 11pm on Sat and Sun Jun-Aug), Oct-Mar 10am-5:30pm.*

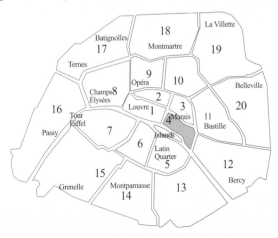

Towers closed Jan 1, May 1, and Dec 25. Free tours in English Wed and Thu at 2pm, Sat at 2:30pm. Admission: Free to the cathedral. Towers: €8, under 18 free. Treasury: €6. www.notredamedeparis.fr.

Centre Georges Pompidou

The Centre Georges Pompidou houses an incredible collection of contemporary art. The building is a work of art in itself. It's "ekoskeletal" (all the plumbing, elevators, and ducts are exposed and brightly painted). This museum has works by Picasso, Matisse, Kandinsky, Pollock, and many other favorite modern artists. *Info: 4th/Métro Rambuteau. place Georges-Pompidou (on rue St-Martin between rue Rambuteau and rue St-Merri). Tel. 01/44.78.12.33. Open Wed-Mon 11am-9pm. Closed Tue and May 1. Admission: To the Center: €13, under 18 free. Free on the first Sun of the month. €3 to visit the 6th floor viewing area. www.cnac-gp.fr.*

place des Vosges

The most beautiful square in Paris, in France, and probably in all of Europe. It's the oldest square in Paris, a beautiful and quiet park surrounded by stone and red-brick houses. Upscale boutiques are found in the attractive arcades. The square is also known as *la place Royale*, as it was designed for royal festivities. Don't miss it! At the square is the **Maison de Victor Hugo** (Victor Hugo's House). You can't seem to go anywhere in this city without seeing the name of Victor Hugo (he wrote *Les Misérables* and *The Hunchback of Notre Dame*). This 19th-century literary legend's home is now a museum. Hugo was also an artist, and you can view 350 of his drawings here. *Info: 4th/Métro St-Paul or Bastille. 6 place des Vosges. Tel. 01/42.72.10.16. Open Tue-Sun 10am-6pm. Closed Mon. Admission: Free.*

The Marais is home to a thriving Jewish community. **Rue des Rosiers** is a great place to get a falafel sandwich and to view shop windows filled with Jewish artifacts.

RESTAURANTS & WINE BARS
L'Ange 20

Don't miss this small, intimate restaurant in the heart of the Marais near the Centre Pompidou. Friendly, efficient, and attentive service. You can watch the chef in the open kitchen. Lively mix of tourists and Parisians enjoying reasonably priced meals. Try the excellent *agneau façon sept heures* (lamb cooked for seven hours). Unbelievable what the chef turns out in this small kitchen.

Info: *4th/Métro Rambuteau. 8 rue Geoffroy L'Angevin (off of rue Beaubourg). Tel. 01/40.27.93.67. No lunch. Closed Mon. www.lange20.com. Moderate.*

Bistrot de L'Oulette

Intimate bistro in the Marais (near the place des Vosges) featuring the specialties of Southwest France (especially *confit de canard*). *Info*: *4th/Métro Bastille. 38 rue des Tournelles (near rue du Pas-de-la-Mule). Tel. 01/42.71.43.33. Closed Sat (lunch) and Sun. www.l-oulette.com. Moderate.*

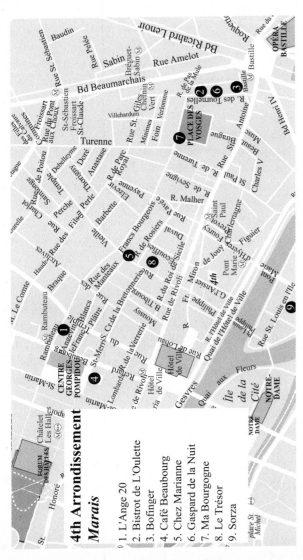

4th Arrondissement
Marais

1. L'Ange 20
2. Bistrot de L'Oulette
3. Bofinger
4. Café Beaubourg
5. Chez Marianne
6. Gaspard de la Nuit
7. Ma Bourgogne
8. Le Trésor
9. Sorza

Ma Bourgogne *Historic Restaurant*
This café/restaurant in the place des Vosges (the oldest square in Paris) serves traditional Parisian cuisine and specializes in *poulet rôti* (roast chicken). Good salads. Open for breakfast, lunch, and dinner. *Info: 4th/Métro St-Paull. 19 place des Vosges. Tel. 01/42.78.44.64. Open daily. No credit cards. www.mabourgogne.fr. Moderate.*

Sorza
This small, modern Italian restaurant with stark red-and-black decor is located on the lovely Île St-Louis. Try the *filet de volaille aux morilles et fetuccine* (chicken fillet with morels and fetuccine) and end with the sinfully rich *mousse au chocolat* (chocolate mousse). *Info: 4th/Métro Pont-Marie. 51 rue Saint-Louis-en-I'lle (on the Île St-Louis). Tel. 01/43.54.78.62. Open daily. Moderate.*

Bofinger *Historic Restaurant*
Beautiful glass-roofed brasserie with lots of stained glass and brass, located between the place des Vosges and the place de la Bastille. It's the oldest Alsatian brasserie in Paris, and still serves traditional dishes like *choucroute* (sauerkraut) and large platters of shellfish. Across the street and less expensive is **Le Petit Bofinger**, *6 rue de la Bastille, Tel. 01/42.72.05.23. Info: 4th/Métro Bastille. 5 rue de la Bastille. Tel. 01/42.72.87.82. Open daily until 1am. www.bofingerparis. com. Moderate-Expensive.*

Gaspard de la Nuit
This cozy restaurant is located in the Marais between the place de la Bastille and place des Vosges. Traditional French cuisine. Try the delicious *carré d'agneau en croûte d'herbs* (loin of lamb with herbs). Always an enjoyable experience. *Info: 4th/Métro Bastille. 6 rue des Tournelles (near rue du Pas-de-la-Mule). Tel. 01/42.77.90.53. Open daily. No lunch. www.legaspard.fr. Moderate-Expensive.*

Chez Marianne *Historic Restaurant*
Popular take-away deli (you can also eat here, but it's difficult to get a table) known for its authentic Jewish and Eastern European specialties, especially falafel. Located in the heart of the Marais. *Info: 4th/Métro St-Paul. 2 rue des Hospitalières-St-Gervais (at rue des Rosiers). Tel. 01/42.72.18.86. Open daily. No credit cards. Inexpensive.*

CAFÉS, TEA SHOPS & COCKTAILS
Café Beaubourg
Looking onto the Centre Pompidou and packed with an artsy crowd. *Info: 4th/Métro Rambuteau. 100 rue Saint-Martin. Tel. 01/48.87.63.96. Open daily 8am to midnight.*

Le Trésor
Cocktails served both inside and outside at tables along this lovely, flowered street in the heart of the Marais. Great people-watching. *Info: 4th/Métro Hôtel de Ville or Saint-Paul. 5-7 rue du Trésor (off of rue Vieille du Temple). Tel. 01/42.71.35.17. Open daily.*

Dammann Frères
Are you a secret tea-totaller? This tea shop is located on the place des Vosges. Walk in and you will find yourself surrounded by walls lined with shelves holding black canisters filled with rare teas, which you can sample before you purchase. The elegant boxes make great gifts or souvenirs. *Info: 4th/Métro St-Paul or Bastille. 15 place des Vosges. Tel. 01/44.54.04.88. Open daily. www.dammann.fr.*

MORE COOKING CLASSES

La Cuisine Paris offers cooking classes in English with themes such as "Parisian Lunch Time" and "Chocolate Delight." *Info: 4th/Métro Hôtel de Ville. 80 Quai de l' Hôtel de Ville. Tel. 01/40.51.78.18. Average cost is about €65. Reservations can be made through their helpful website www.lacuisineparis.com.*

5ᴿᴰ ARRONDISSEMENT
Latin Quarter

The 5th, south of Île de la Cité on the Left Bank of the Seine, is home to the Quartier Latin (Latin Quarter). It's a maze of small streets and squares surrounding La Sorbonne, the famous university. The name Latin Quarter comes from the university tradition of speaking and studying in Latin.

SIGHTS

Musée de Cluny (Musée National du Moyen Age/Thermesde Cluny). The building that houses this museum (the Hôtel de Cluny) has had many lives. It's been a Roman bathhouse in the 3rd century (you can still visit the ruins downstairs), a mansion for a religious abbot in the 15th century, a royal residence, and since 1844, a museum. It's a must if you're interested in medieval arts and crafts. Chalices, manuscripts, crosses, vestments, carvings, sculptures, and the acclaimed *Lady and the Unicorn* tapestries are all here. You enter through the cobblestoned *Cour d'Honneur* (Court of Honor) surrounded by a Gothic building with gargoyles and turrets. There's also a lovely medieval garden. *Info: 5th/Métro Cluny-La Sorbonne. 6 place Paul-Painlevé. Tel. 01/53.73.78.16. Open Tue-Sun 9:15am-5:45pm. Closed Tue. Admission: €8.50, under 18 free. Free the first Sun of the month. www.musee-moyenage.fr.*

If medieval arts and crafts are not your thing, head east down boulevard St-Germain-des-Prés. At the river you'll find the **Institut du Monde Arabe**

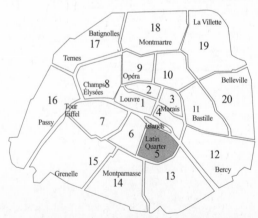

(Arab World Institute). This museum of architecture, photography, decorative arts and religion is devoted to providing insight into the Arab world. The modern building in which the museum is housed has striking traditional Arabic geometry etched into the windows. *Info: 5th/Métro Jussieu. 1 rue des Fossés-St-Bernard. Tel. 01/40.51.38.38. Open Tue-Sun 10am-6pm (Fri until 9:30pm, Sat and Sun until 7pm). Closed Mon. Admission: Museum: €8, under 18 free. www.imarabe.org.*

If you're interested in French history, then you may want to head to the **Panthéon**. Originally a church, it's now the burial place for some of the greats of French history, including Voltaire, Victor Hugo, Louis Braille (who created the language for the blind) and Marie Curie (the only woman buried here). Notice the giant frescoes of the life of St. Geneviève. *Info: 5th/ Métro Cardinal Lemoine. place du Panthéon. Tel. 01/44.32.18.00. Open daily 10am-6pm. Admission: €8, under 18 free.*

The **Jardin des Plantes** is a quiet park not frequented by many travelers. It's especially known for its herb garden. The zoo here (the *Ménagerie*) is one of the oldest in the world. *Info: 5th/Métro Jussieu. Off of the Quai St-Bernard, west of Gare d'Austerlitz. Tel. 01/40.79.56.01. Open daily 8am-5:30pm (until 7:45pm in summer). Admission: Free (gardens), €10 (zoo), under 4 free.* Also at the park is the **Musée National d'Histoire Naturelle** (National Museum of Natural History). Visit the Gallery of the Evolution of Man and exhibits on everything from entomology (the study of insects) to paleontology (the study of dinosaurs). You'll be greeted by a huge whale skeleton. (You may want to skip the skeletons of fetuses and Siamese twins.) *Info: 5th/Métro Jussieu. 36 rue Geoffroy St-Hilaire. Tel. 01/40.79.56.01. Open 10am-6pm. Closed Tue. Admission: €7, €under 26 free.*

Nearby is the **Mosquée de Paris**, modeled after the Alhambra in Spain. This pink mosque was built in the 1920s as a tribute to Muslims from North Africa who supported France in World War I. It's the spiritual center for Muslims in Paris. There's a tea room, a school, and Turkish baths on the premises. *Info: 5th/Métro Monge. 2b place du Puits-de-l'Ermite. Tel. 01/45.35.97.33. Open 9am-noon and 2pm-6pm. Closed Fridays and Islamic holidays. Admission: €3.*

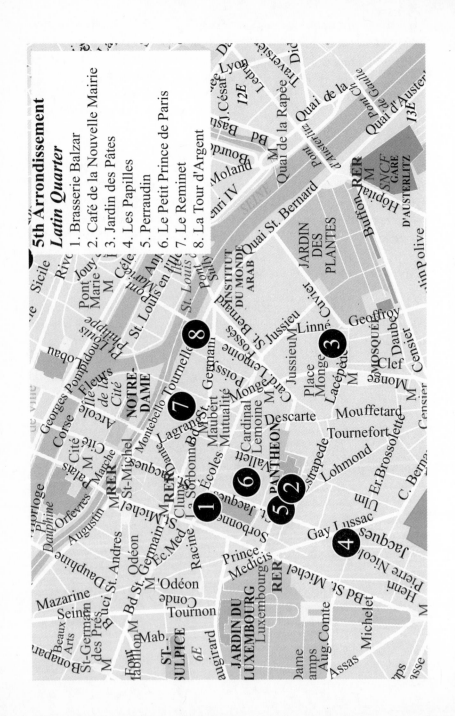

5th Arrondissement
Latin Quarter

1. Brasserie Balzar
2. Café de la Nouvelle Mairie
3. Jardin des Pâtes
4. Les Papilles
5. Perraudin
6. Le Petit Prince de Paris
7. Le Reminet
8. La Tour d'Argent

RESTAURANTS & WINE BARS

Brasserie Balzar *Historic Restaurant*
This Latin Quarter brasserie opened in 1898 and serves traditional French cuisine. It's known for its *poulet rôti* (roast chicken), onion soup and "colorful" waiters. *Info: 5th/Métro Cluny-La Sorbonne. 49 rue des Ecoles (near blvd. Saint-Michel). Tel. 01/43.54.13.67. Open daily until midnight. www.brasseriebalzar. com. Moderate-Expensive.*

Le Reminet
This quaint bistro is located in the Latin Quarter near St-Michel and just across the river from Notre-Dame. Helpful staff and the romantic atmosphere (down to candelabras on the tables) make for a wonderful evening. Start with a *kir royal* (an aperitif made with champagne and creme de cassis). Try the *piccatta de veau* (veal piccatta) or *pot-au-feu* (a stew of meat and vegetables). Good wine list featuring wines from all French regions. *Info: 5th/Métro Maubert-Mutualité or St-Michel. 5 rue des Grands-Degrés (one block south of Quai de la Tournelle at rue Mâitre-Albert). Tel. 01/44.07.04.24. Open daily. www.lereminet.com. Moderate-Expensive.*

Les Papilles
Near the Panthéon – the name means Tastebuds – this restaurant sells gourmet foods and wine, and offers creative takes on French cuisine. Try the tender hanger steak. Worth the trip! *Info: 5th/Métro Cluny-La Sorbonne (RER Luxembourg). 30 rue Gay-Lussac (near rue Saint-Jacques). Tel. 01/43.25.20.79. Closed Sun, Mon and part of Aug. www.lespapillesparis. fr. Moderate.*

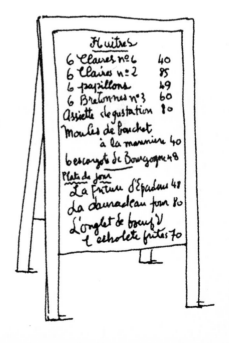

Le Petit Prince de Paris
Walk through the velvet curtains and enter the intimate dining room at this funky, fun, and friendly bistro near the Sorbonne. There are several *prix-fixe* (fixed-priced) menus. Try

the *magret de canard* (breast of fattened duck). Fantastic chocolate desserts. *Info:* 5th/Métro Maubert-Mutualité. 12 rue de Lanneau (near rue des Ecoles). Tel. 01/43.54.77.26. Open daily for dinner. www.lepetitprincedeparis.fr. Moderate.

Perraudin *Historic Restaurant*
You'll get to know your fellow diners at this inexpensive bistro serving traditional Parisian cuisine just steps from the Panthéon. Try the *magret de canard au miel et romarin* (duck breast with honey and rosemary sauce). *Info:* 5th/Métro Cluny-La Sorbonne. 157 rue Saint-Jacques (near rue Soufflot). Tel. 01/46.33.15.75. No reservations. Open daily. www.restaurant-perraudin.com. Inexpensive-Moderate.

Café de la Nouvelle Mairie
This bustling wine bar/café near the Panthéon serves classic French food and small plates. There are about twenty wines served by the glass (starting at €4) and many are organic. Especially nice in the summer. Friendly English-speaking staff. Always packed elbow-to-elbow. *Info:* 5th/Métro Cardinal Lemoine or RER B Luxembourg. 19 rue des Fossés Saint Jacques. Tel. 01/44.07.04.41. Closed most weekends. Inexpensive-Moderate.

La Tour d'Argent *Historic Restaurant*
The dining room of this famous and award-winning restaurant has an excellent view of Notre-Dame and the Seine River. Duck is the specialty, and the restaurant raises them on its own farm. You'll receive a postcard with the duck's serial number if you choose to order the house specialty. The restaurant's wine cellar is said to have 450,000 bottles. The wine list contains 15,000 wines on a 400-page list. An incredible experience at an incredible price. *Info:* 5th/Métro Maubert-Mutualité. 15-17 quai de la Tournelle. Tel. 01/43.54.23.31. www.latourdargent.com. Very Expensive.

Jardin des Pâtes
Pâtes means pasta. The pasta at this restaurant, near the Jardin des Plantes, is made fresh daily on the premises. Pasta choices include wheat, buckwheat, rye, barley, rice, and chestnut. Both the duck breast and salmon dishes are popular. A nice change of pace if you've eaten traditional French cuisine for a few days in a row. Lots of vegetarian choices. *Info:* 5th/Métro Place Monge. 4 rue Lacépède (between rue Linné and rue Monge). Tel. 01/43.31.50.71. Open daily. Inexpensive-Moderate.

6ᵀᴴ ARRONDISSEMENT
Saint-Germain

The 5th and 6th, south of Île de la Cité on the Left Bank of the Seine, is home to the Quartier Latin (Latin Quarter). It's a maze of small streets and squares surrounding La Sorbonne, the famous university. The name Latin Quarter comes from the university tradition of speaking and studying in Latin.

SIGHTS

Jardin du Luxembourg

The Jardin du Luxembourg (Luxembourg Gardens) are famous, formal French gardens filled with locals and tourists. Lots of children around the pond playing with wooden sailboats. There's a replica of the Statue of Liberty in the western part of the gardens. The Statue of Liberty in New York was a gift from the French. Also here is the **Palais du Luxembourg** (Luxembourg Palace), the home of the French Senate. Tours of the palace are by reservation only. The **Musée du Luxembourg** at 19 rue Vaugirard occupies a wing of the Palais du Luxembourg and features temporary exhibitions of some of the big names in the history of art. *Info for museum: Tel. 01/40.13.62.00. Open daily 10am-7:30pm (until 10pm on Fri and Mon) Admission: Depends on the exhibit, but usually €11, under 13 free. Info for gardens: 6ᵗʰ/Métro Cluny-La Sorbonne. A few blocks south of boulevard St-Germain-des-Prés (off of the boulevard St Michel). Admission: Free.*

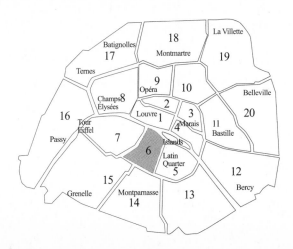

The **Eglise St-Sulpice**, located on an attractive square with a lovely fountain (the **Fontaine-des-Quatre Points**), has one of the largest pipe organs in the world with over 6,700 pipes. You'll notice that one of the two bell towers was never completed. Inside are frescoes by Delacroix in the Chapel of the Angels (*Chapelle des Anges*), a statue of the Virgin and child by Pigalle, and Servandoni's Chapel of the Madonna (*Chapelle de la Madone*). Set into the floor of the aisle of the north-south transept is a bronze line. On the two equinoxes and the winter solstice, the sun reflects onto a globe and obelisk and from there to a crucifix. The obelisk reads: "Two scientists with God's help." You may find fans of the wildly popular book *The Da Vinci Code* looking around the church. It was the scene of a brutal killing in the book. *Info: 6th/Métro St-Sulpice. place St-Sulpice (between the boulevard St-Germain-des-Prés and the Luxembourg Gardens). Open daily. Admission: Free.*

The **Eglise St-Germain-des-Prés**, located in the fashionable Left Bank neighborhood that shares its name, dates back to the 6th century. A Gothic choir, 19th-century spire and Romanesque paintings all attest to its long history. It's a frequent and beautiful site for classical concerts. *Info: 6th/Métro St-Germain. place St-Germain-des-Prés. Open daily. Admission: Free.*

RESTAURANTS & WINE BARS
Bouillon Racine *Historic Restaurant*
Brasserie in a historic building with Art Nouveau decor. Try one of the soups offered such as *crème de potiron et châtaigne* (cream of pumpkin and chestnut). *Info: 6th/Métro Cluny-La Sorbonne or Odéon. 3 rue Racine (near blvd. Saint-Michel). Tel. 01/44.32.15.60. Open daily. www.bouillon-raacine. Moderate.*

Le Timbre
The name means "stamp" which is appropriate for this tiny Left Bank bistro. A wonderful Parisian experience. How does the English chef turn out such wonderful dishes in such a small kitchen? Excellent *daube de boeuf* (beef stew). *Info: 6th/Métro Notre-Dame-des-Champs. 3 rue Ste-Beuve (off of rue Notre-Dame-des-Champs). Closed Sun, Mon and part of Aug. Tel. 01/45.49.10.40. www.restauranttimbre. Moderate.*

Polidor *Historic Restaurant*
You'll sit at communal tables at this popular old-fashioned bistro serving traditional cuisine such as *pintade* (guinea hen). French comfort food. *Info: 6th/*

Métro Odéon. 41 rue Monsieur-le-Prince (near rue Racine). Tel. 01/43.26.95.34. Open daily. No reservations. No credit cards. Inexpensive-Moderate.

Fish (La Boissonnerie)

Drew Harre and Juan Sanchez provide a warm welcome. Open for fourteen years, this popular restaurant and wine bar is a great place for a glass of wine. You'll find many English speakers here (everyone who works here appears to speak English). The food is good and reliable. We like to sit at the bar and sample the wines offered by the glass (mostly from smaller wine regions). *Info: 6th/Métro Mabillon. 69 rue de Seine. Tel. 01/43.54.34.69. Moderate.*

Le Relais de l'Entrecôtes

If you're the type that can't decide what to order, here's your restaurant. There's only one thing on the menu: steak. All you need to do is tell them how you want your steak done. (See the helpful tip on how you want your

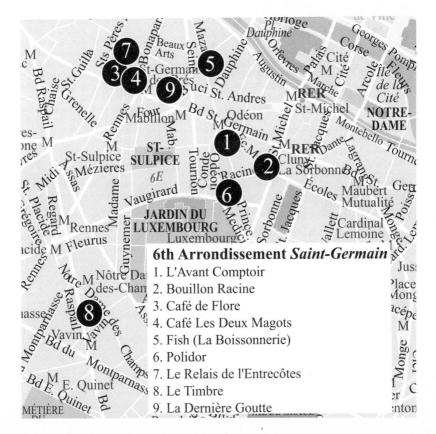

6th Arrondissement *Saint-Germain*

1. L'Avant Comptoir
2. Bouillon Racine
3. Café de Flore
4. Café Les Deux Magots
5. Fish (La Boissonnerie)
6. Polidor
7. Le Relais de l'Entrecôtes
8. Le Timbre
9. La Dernière Goutte

meat cooked on this page.) You'll be served a green salad, followed by your steak (in a secret sauce), and delicious crispy fries. For dessert, try the *crème brûlee*. *Info: 6th/Métro St-Germain-des-Prés. 20 rue Saint-Benoît (off of blvd St-Germain). Tel. 01/45.49.16.00. Open daily noon-3pm and 7pm-11:30pm. Fixed priced lunch and dinner is €26. No reservations. Second location in the 6th/Métro Vavin. 101 blvd. due Montparnasse (at rue Vavin). Tel. 01/46.33.82.82. www.relaisentrecote.fr.*

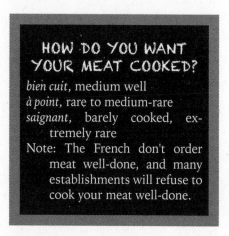

HOW DO YOU WANT
YOUR MEAT COOKED?

bien cuit, medium well
à point, rare to medium-rare
saignant, barely cooked, extremely rare
Note: The French don't order meat well-done, and many establishments will refuse to cook your meat well-done.

L'Avant Comptoir

This narrow, standing-room-only space serves a selection of tasty Basque tapas. You'll share jars of pickles and peppers with your fellow patrons. Try the delicious Iberian ham croquettes and down them with a glass of organic wine. This is a great place to visit after a stroll in the nearby Luxembourg Gardens, but get there early to beat the crowds. *Info: 6th/Métro Odéon. 3 Carrefour de l'Odéon.(off of rue de l'Odéon). No telephone. No reservations. Open daily. Inexpensive-Moderate.*

CAFES

Café Les Deux Magots *Historic Café*

If you're a tourist, you'll fit right in at one of Hemingway's favorite spots. We don't really recommend that you eat here (there is a limited menu), but have a drink and enjoy the great people-watching. *Info: 6th/Métro Saint-Germain-des-Prés. 6 place Saint-Germain-des-Prés. Tel. 01/45.48.55.25. Open daily 7:30am to 1am. www.cafelesdeuxmagots.fr.*

Café de Flore *Historic Café*

Another famous café and a favorite of tourists and Parisians alike (next door to Les Deux Magots). *Info: 6th/Métro Saint-Germain-des-Prés. 172 boulevard. Saint-Germain-des-Prés. Tel. 01/45.48.55.26. Open daily 7am to 2am. www.cafedeflore.fr.*

WINE SHOP
La Dernière Goutte

Located in an old vaulted room. The owners are charming and friendly, and they frequently have wine tastings. The name means "the last drop." The photo on the back cover of this book was taken here. _Info_: *6th/Métro St-Germain-des-Prés. 6 rue de Bourbon-le-Château. Tel. 01/43.29.11.62. www.ladernieregoutte.net.*

7ᵀᴴ ARRONDISSEMENT
Eiffel Tower/Invalides

The chic 7th is home to some of the city's grandest sights, including the Eiffel Tower, Musée d'Orsay and Les Invalides.

SIGHTS
Tour Eiffel (Eiffel Tower)
The Eiffel Tower was called, among other things, an "iron monster" when it was erected. Gustave-Alexandre Eiffel never meant for his 7,000-ton tower to be permanent, and it was almost torn down. Today, it's without a doubt the most recognizable structure in the world. You can either take the elevator or climb the 1,652 stairs. You cannot visit Paris without a trip to this incredible structure. Across the Seine River from the Eiffel Tower, are the **Jardins du Trocadéro** (Trocadéro Gardens), home to the **Palais de Chaillot**. This huge palace is surrounded by more than 60 fountains. _Info: 7ᵗʰ/Métro Trocadéro, École Militaire or Bir-Hakeim. Champ-de-Mars. Tel. 892 70 00 16. Open daily. Elevator: 9:30am-11:45pm (final ascension 10:30pm to the top). From mid-June to end of Aug 9am-12:45am (final ascension 11pm to the top). Stairs: 9:30am-6:30pm (last admission 6pm). From mid-June to end of Aug 9am-12:45am (last admission midnight). Admission to the second landing by stairs: €5, 24-12 years €3.50, 11-4 €3, under 4 free. Admission to the second landing by elevator: €8.50, 24-12 years €7, 11-4 €4, under 4 free. Elevator to the top: €14, 24-12 years, €12.50, 11-4 €9.50, under 4 free. www.toureiffel.fr._

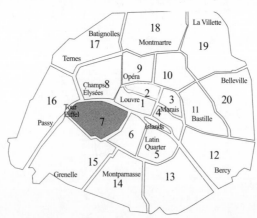

Musée d'Orsay

The Musée d'Orsay is located across the Seine from the Tuileries and the Louvre in a former train station that has been gloriously converted into 80 galleries. Many of the most famous Impressionist and Post-Impressionist works are here. There are works by Whistler, Manet, Dega, Renoir, Monet, Sargent, Pissaro and van Gogh, just to name a few. *Info: 7ᵗʰ/Métro Solférino. 1 rue de la Légion d'Honneur. Tel. 01/40.49.48.14. Open Tue-Sun 9:00am-6pm (Thu until 9:45pm). Last ticket sold at 5:00pm (9:00pm Thu). Closed Mon, Jan 1, May 1 and Dec 25. Admission: €12, €9.50 ages 18-25, under 18 free. €9.50 after 4:30pm (after 6pm on Thu). Free the first Sun of each month. www.musee-orsay.fr.*

Hôtel des Invalides

The Hôtel des Invalides was built in 1670 for disabled soldiers. The world's greatest military museum, **Musée de l'Armée** (Army Museum), is here, as is the second-tallest monument in Paris, the **Eglise du Dôme** (Dome Church). The main attraction here is **Napoléon's Tomb**, an enormous red stone sarcophagus. *Info: 7ᵗʰ/Métro Invalides or La Tour-Maubourg. 129 rue de Grenelle. Tel. 01/44.42.38.77. Open daily Nov-Mar 10am-5pm, Apr-Oct 10am-6pm. Closed first Mon of each month (except Jul- Sep) and Jan 1, May 1, Nov 1, Dec 25. The Dome is open until 7pm in Jul and Aug. Admission: €9, under 18 free. www.invalides.org.*

Musée Rodin

Rodin is the father of modern sculpture and is known for his sculptures of giant-muscled nudes. This museum is in Rodin's former studio, an 18ᵗʰ-century mansion with a beautiful rose garden. His best-known work, *The Thinker*, is here, along with many other major works. *Info: 7ᵗʰ/Métro Varenne. 77 rue de Varenne. Tel. 01/44.18.61.10. Open Tue-Sun 10am-5:45pm (Wed until 8:45pm). Closed Mon. Closed Jan 1, May 1, and Dec 25. Admission: €9, €5 ages 18-25, under 18 free. €1 (garden only). Free on the first Sun of the month. www.musee-rodin.fr.*

Musée Maillol (Fondation Dina Vierny-Musée Maillol)

This museum's permanent collection includes works of Aristide Maillol, a contemporary of Matisse, along with rare sketches by Picasso, Cézanne, Degas and other 20th-century artists. The museum also features revolving exhibits of some of the world's best-known artists. *Info: 7th/Métro Rue du*

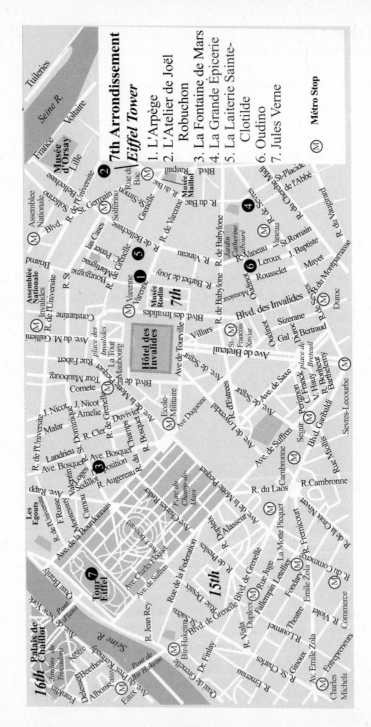

7th Arrondissement
Eiffel Tower

1. L'Arpège
2. L'Atelier de Joël Robuchon
3. La Fontaine de Mars
4. La Grande Épicerie
5. La Laiterie Sainte-Clotilde
6. Oudino
7. Jules Verne

Ⓜ **Métro Stop**

Bac. 59-61 rue de Grenelle. Tel. 01/42.22.59.58. Open daily 10:30am-7pm (Fri until 9:30pm). Admission: €11, under 11 free. www.museemaillol.com.

RESTAURANTS & WINE BARS

La Fontaine de Mars

Red-checked tablecloths and friendly service near the Eiffel Tower. Try the *poulet fermier aux morilles* (free-range chicken with morel mushrooms). Prices have increased quite a bit since the Obamas ate here. Still, highly recommended. *Info: 7th/Métro Ecole-Militaire. 129 rue St-Dominique (near Avenue Bosquet). Tel. 01/47.05.46.44. Open daily. www.fontainedemars.com. Moderate.*

La Laiterie Sainte-Clotilde

The blackboard menu features French comfort food. You'll dine (in a former milk and cheese shop) with a chic local crowd. A down-to-earth bistro in an expensive neighborhood (not too far from the Musée d'Orsay). Try the *oeufs meurette* (poached eggs in red wine sauce) or the tasty *blanquette de veau* (veal stew). *Info: 7th/Métro Solférino or Rue du Bac. 64 rue de Bellechasse (off of rue de Grenelle). Tel. 01/45.51.74.61. Closed Sun. Moderate.*

Oudino

This bistro is located on an attractive small street. You can start your meal with a *salade caesar* (Caesar salad) and dine on excellent *entrecôte* served with a *béarnaise* sauce. A real find. *Info: 7th/Métro Vaneau. 17 rue Oudinot (off of blvd. des Invalides). Tel. 01/45.66.05.09. Closed Sat (lunch) and Sun. www.oudino.fr. Moderate.*

WINE SHOP

La Grande Épicerie

The ultimate grocery store (with wine cellar and carry-out). Even if you have been here before, you must return to see this incredible wine store and restaurant. *Le plus beau cave du vin du monde* (the most beautiful wine cellar in the world)! *Info: 7th/Métro Sèvres Babylone. 38 rue Sèvres (in the Le Bon Marché department store). Tel. 01/44.39.81.00. Closed Sun.*

COOKING CLASS

Former New York chef & caterer Richard Nahem, and chef and caterer Charlotte Puckette, conduct the **Eye Prefer Paris** cooking classes. Classes start at 9am by shopping at a fresh food market. Then, you head to Charlotte's private townhouse located in the 7th arrondissement, near the Eiffel Tower.

After students arrive, they discuss the menu with Charlotte over coffee and then prepare a five-course feast for the next few hours. The meal is then shared, accompanied by French wine from a local wine shop. Classes end at approximately 2pm. _Info:_ _€185. Tue, Wed, Thu, and Fri. Minimum of 2 students, maximum of 6. www.eyepreferparistours.com/cooking-class._

FAMOUS RESTAURANTS/FAMOUS CHEFS

The 7th arrondissement is home to several award-winning restaurants with impressive wine lists. These restaurants are very expensive and highly praised. Reservations well in advance are a must, as are jacket and tie.

L'Arpège
7th/Métro Varenne, 84 rue de Varenne, Tel. 01/47.05.09.06, www.alain-passard.com.
The emphasis is on vegetables at Alain Passard's award-winning restaurant.

L'Atelier de Joël Robuchon
7th/Métro Rue du Bac, 5 rue de Montalembert, Tel. 01/42.22.56.56, www.joel-rubuchon.net.
Joël Robuchon presents fine dining in a relaxed setting. You'll dine with others at seats surrounding U-shaped bars. Reservations only for first sitting.

Jules Verne
7th/Métro Bir-Hakeim, Second level of the Eiffel Tower, Tel. 01/45.55.61.44, www.lejulesverne-paris.com.
Alain Ducasse has taken over this incredible restaurant with an extraordinary location on the second level of the Eiffel Tower.

8ᵀᴴ ARRONDISSEMENT
Arc de Triomphe/Champs-Élysées

Luxurious shopping, the place de la Concorde, the Champs-Élysées and the Arc de Triomphe are all found in the 8th.

SIGHTS
Arc de Triomphe

The Arc de Triomphe is the largest triumphal arch in the world. Napoléon commissioned it in 1806 and it was completed in 1836. The Arc is the home to the Tomb of the Unknown Soldier, and is engraved with the names of generals in Napoléon's victories. There's an observation deck providing one of the greatest views of Paris. If you aren't impressed by the view down the Champs-Élysées, you really shouldn't have come to Paris. *Info: 8ᵗʰ/Métro Charles-de-Gaulle-Étoile. place Charles-de-Gaulle-Étoile. Tel. 01/55.37.73.77. Open daily Apr-Sep 10am-11pm, Oct-Mar 10:00am-10:30pm. Closed on January 1, May 1, May 8 (morning) July 14 (morning), November 11 (morning) and December 25. Admission: €9.50, €5 ages 18-25, under 18 free. www. arcdetriompheparis.com.*

Avenue des Champs-Élysées

The Avenue des Champs-Élysées is one of the most famous streets in the world. It's home to expensive retail shops, fast-food chains, car dealers, banks, huge movie theatres and overpriced cafés. You can sit at a café and experience great people-watching.

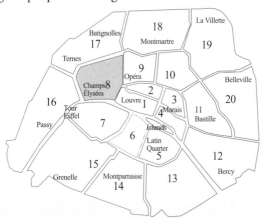

On the edge of beautiful **Parc Monceau** is the **Musée Cernuschi**. Cernuschi was a banker from Milan who bequeathed his lovely home and incredible collection of Asian art to the city. A must for Asian-art aficionados. There's also a collection of Persian bronze objects. Explanatory map and notes are in English. *Info: 8th/Métro Monceau. 7 avenue Vélasquez. Tel. 01/53.96.21.50. Open 10am-6pm. Closed Mon. Admission: Free. www.cernuschi.paris.fr.*

The **Musée Nissim de Camondo** is dedicated to 18th-century objets d'art and furniture. Located in a mansion overlooking the beautiful Parc Monceau, it showcases objects owned by such notables as Marie-Antoinette. The kitchen of the mansion has been painstakingly restored. *Info: 8th/Métro Monceau. 63 rue de Monceau. Tel. 01/53.89.06.50. Open Wed-Sun 10am-5:30pm. Closed Mon-Tue. Admission: €8, under 18 free.*

The area around the **place de la Madeleine** (8th/Métro Madeleine)is packed with fabulous specialty-food shops (the windows of the food store Fauchon are worth a trip by themselves), wine dealers, restaurants, and tea rooms. This is a perfect place for eating and purchasing culinary souvenirs. There's something for every taste- but this is an upscale area, and can be expensive. Note that most stores on the square are closed on Sunday. The church in the middle of this square is the **Eglise de la Madeleine**. This neo-Classical church has 52 Corinthian columns and provides a great view (from the top of the monumental steps) of the place de la Concorde. Huge bronze doors depicting the Ten Commandments provide the impressive entry to the light-filled marble interior. There are three giant domes and a huge pipe organ. The painting in the chancel depicts the history of Christianity. Such grand events as the funerals of Chopin and Coco Chanel (now there's a pair!) were held here. *Info: 8th/Métro Madeleine. place de la Madeleine. Open daily. Admission: Free.*

Among the department stores and shops on boulevard Haussmann is the **Musée Jacquemart-André** featuring art, especially from the Italian Renaissance. Jacquemart and André collected rare paintings and decorative art in this 1850s mansion. Although the museum with its paintings by Rembrandt, Bellini, Carpaccio, Van Dyck and Rubens is memorable, the opulent mansion is the real star here. Marble staircases, chandeliers and elaborately painted ceilings vie for your attention rather than the paintings on the walls. The high-ceilinged dining room, with its 18th-century tapestries, is a popular place to rest and have tea, a salad or pastry. *Info: 8th/Métro*

Miromesnil. 158 boulevard Haussmann. Tel. 01/45.62.11.59. Open daily 10am-6pm. Café open daily 11:45am-5:30pm. Admission: €11, under 7 free. www.musee-jacquemart-andre.com.

RESTAURANTS & WINE BARS

Wining and dining in the 8th arrondissement is not cheap. The restaurants below are very expensive and highly praised. All have impressive and award-winning wine lists. Reservations well in advance are a must, as are jacket and tie.

Alain Ducasse

Restaurant Plaza Athénée, 8th/Métro Alma-Marceau, 25 avenue Montaigne, Tel. 01/53.67.65.00, www.alain-ducasse.com.

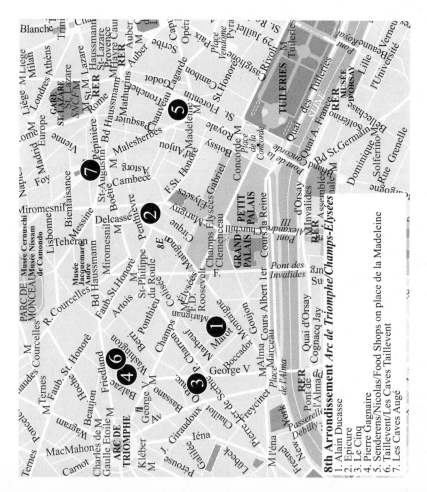

Le Bristol (Epicure), *8th/Métro Miromesnil, 112 rue du Faubourg St-Honoré, Tel. 01/53.43.43.40, www.lebristolparis.com.*

Le Cinq, *8th/Métro George V, 31 avenue George V (in the Four Seasons George V), Tel. 01/49.52.71.54, www.fourseasons.com/paris.*

Pierre Gagnaire, *8th/Métro George V, 6 rue Balzac (Hôtel Balzac), Tel. 01/58.36.12.50, www.pierre-gagnaire.com.*

Senderens, *8th/Métro Madeleine, 9 place de la Madeleine, Tel. 01/42.65.22.90, www.senderens.fr.*

Taillevent, *8th/Métro George V, 15 rue Lamennais, Tel. 01/44.95.15.01, www. taillevent.com.*

WINE SHOPS
Les Caves Taillevent
This wine shop is associated with the well-known Taillevent restaurant and is said to have over 500,000 bottles of wine starting at around €5. You'll be amazed at the cost of some selections. *Info: 8th/Métro Charles-de-Gaulle-Étoile or Saint-Philippe-du-Roule. 199 rue du Faubourg-Saint-Honoré. Tel. 01/45.61.14.09. Open Tue-Sat 10am-7:30pm. Closed Sun and Aug. www. taillevent.com.*

Nicolas
Located upstairs from the Nicolas wine shop. You can buy a bottle of wine at the shop and have it served with your meal. The menu is limited, but the wines sold by the glass are inexpensive. *Info: 8th/Métro Madeleine at 31 place de la Madeleine. Tel. 01/42.68.00.16 Open Mon-Sat 9:30pm-8pm. www. nicolas-wines.com. Over 200 wine stores located throughout Paris.*

Les Caves Augé
Famous wine shop since 1850 offering everything from prestige wines to foreign vintages. *Info: 8th/Métro Saint-Augustin. 116 boulevard Haussmann. Tel. 01/45.22.16.97. Closed Sun and Mon (morning).*

FOOD SHOPS

You'll find some of the most interesting food shops in the world around the **place de la Madeleine** in the 8th arrondissement.

- **Boutique Maille** (number 6). Boutique mustard shop.

- **L'Ecluse** (number 15). Chain of wine bars. Not the greatest food in Paris, but great for wine tasting (especially Bordeaux).

- **Caviar Kaspia** (number 17). Caviar, blinis and salmon. There's also a restaurant upstairs.

- **Hédiard** (number 21). Food store/spice shop that's been open since the 1850s, similar to Fauchon, with an on-site restaurant.

- **Nicolas** (number 31). Located upstairs from the Nicolas wine shop. You can buy a bottle of wine at the shop and have it served with your meal. The menu is limited, but the wines sold by the glass are inexpensive.

- **Fauchon** (number 26). Deli and grocery known for its huge selection of canned food, baked goods and alcohol. The store is a must for those wanting to bring back French specialties.

- **La Maison du Miel** (located around the corner from Fauchon at 24 rue Vignon). This food store contains everything made from honey (from sweets to soap).

- **Marquise de Sévigné** (number 32). A French "luxury" (their word) chocolate maker since 1898.

9ᵀᴴ ARRONDISSEMENT
Opéra

Home to the opulent Opéra Garnier, a center for shopping (most major department stores are here), and a mecca for nightlife.

SIGHTS

On the square (the **place de l'Opéra**) is the **Opéra Garnier**. Built in 1875, this ornate opera house is now the showplace for both opera and dance. It's often referred to as the most opulent theater in the world. Chandeliers, marble stairways, red-velvet boxes, a ceiling painted by Chagall, and a facade of marble and sculpture make this the perfect place for an elegant night out in Paris. There's also a museum celebrating opera and dance over the years. *Info: 9th/Métro Opéra. place de l'Opéra. Tel. 01/71.25.24.23. Open daily 10am-5pm. Admission: €9, under 10 free.*

Nearby is the **Musée de la Parfumerie-Fragonard**. Located in a lovely 1860 town house, this museum is devoted to the history of perfume from the time of the Egyptians to today. *Info: 9th/Métro Opéra. 9 rue Scribe. Tel. 01/47.42.04.56. Open Mon-Sat 9am-6pm (Sunday until 5pm). Admission: Free.*

If you're not into opera or perfume, visit **Paris-Story**. Okay, so it's really touristy. This 45-minute multimedia show is a good introduction to what Paris has to offer and is an interesting educational experience (especially for children), as it highlights the history of the city. Headphones provide

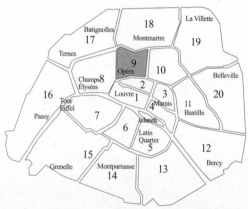

translations in 12 languages. *Info: 9th/Métro Opéra. 11 bis rue Scribe. Tel. 01/42.66.62.06. Open daily. Shows hourly 10am-6pm. Admission: €10.50, €6.30 ages 6-18, under 6 free, families (two adults and two children €27.30. www.paris-story.com.*

Just off the place de l'Opéra is the **place Vendôme**. This elegant square is the home of a 144-foot column honoring Napoléon. You'll find world-famous jewelers here, and great shopping for those with lots of disposable income.

Boulevard Haussmann (just off the place de l'Opéra) is the home to the top two department stores in Paris. **Galeries Lafayette** (*40 blvd. Haussmann, 9th/Métro Chaussée d'Antin*) opened in 1894. You'll find designer clothes, a wonderful food hall and a free view of Paris from the 7th floor. **Au Printemps** (*64 blvd. Haussmann, 9th/Métro Havre-Caumartin*) opened in 1864. Here, you'll find designer clothing, household goods and furniture. The tearoom on the 6th floor has a stained-glass ceiling. Two levels are devoted to beauty supplies and treatments. Which is better? You decide. Both are closed most Sundays and open late on Thursdays.

One other museum of note near here is the **Musée de la Vie Romantique**. Housed in an Italianate villa, the first floor showcases the personal effects of novelist George Sand, including her watercolors. The second floor is devoted to the collection of painter Ary Scheffer of the Romantic movement (from which the museum takes its name). The museum is lovely, especially the garden and greenhouse. *Info: 9th/Métro Blanche. 16 rue Chaptal. Tel. 01/55.31.95.67. Open 10am-6pm. Closed Mon. Admission: Permanent collection is free.*

RESTAURANTS & WINE BARS
Bistro des Deux Théâtres
Affordable dining at this neighborhood bistro near the place de Clichy. Excellent *foie gras de canard* (fattened duck liver). *Info: 9th/Métro Trinité. 18 rue Blanche (at rue Moncey). Tel. 01/45.26.41.43. Open daily. www.bistrocie.fr. Moderate.*

Au Petit Riche
This classic bistro, with authentic 1880s decor, serves specialties of the Loire Valley with a Parisian twist. Try the *vol-au vent de ris de veau* (puff pastry filled with veal sweetbreads). *Info: 9th/Métro Le Peletier or Richelieu-Drouot. 25 rue Le Peletier (at rue Rossini). Tel. 01/47.70.68.68. Open daily. www.aupetitriche. Moderate.*

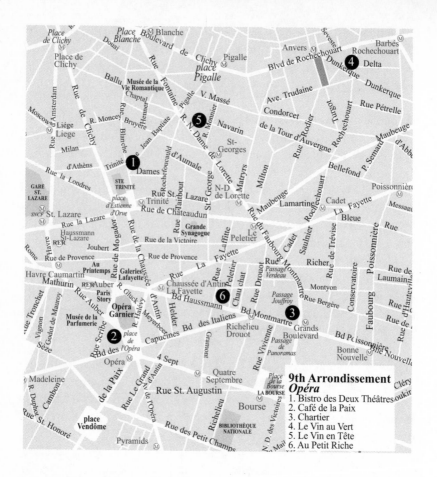

9th Arrondissement
Opéra
1. Bistro des Deux Théâtres
2. Café de la Paix
3. Chartier
4. Le Vin au Vert
5. Le Vin en Tête
6. Au Petit Riche

Chartier *Historic Restaurant*
Traditional Paris soup kitchen. The *tripes à la mode de Caen* is a frequent special of the day (we passed on that). Lots of tourists, and you may be seated with strangers. Expect to wait in line. You're coming here for the experience, not necessarily for the food. *Info: 9th/Métro Grands Boulevards. 7 rue du Faubourg-Montmartre (off of blvd. Poissonnière). Tel. 01/47.70.86.29. Open daily 11:30am to 10pm. www.restaurant-chartier.com. Inexpensive.*

Le Vin au Vert
Small plates (hot and cold) at this casual and friendly wine bar located south of Sacré-Coeur. The food is simple and uncomplicated. There's an emphasis on organic wines. *Info: 9th/Métro Anvers. 70 rue de Dunkerque. Tel. 01/83.56.46.93. Closed Sun and Mon. Inexpensive-Moderate.*

CAFÉ
Café de la Paix *Historic Café*
Famous café (not really known for its food). Popular with tourists. Another spot for outdoor people-watching (and the inside is beautiful). *Info: 9th/Métro Opéra. 12 boulevard des Capucines (place de l'Opéra). Tel. 01/40.07.36.36. Open daily 7am to midnight. www.cafedelapaix.fr.*

WINE SHOP
Le Vin en Tête
This wine shop offers wines from all of France's regions and a selection of foreign wines, and specializes in organic wines. You can also visit them in the 17th/Métro Rome or Place du Clichy. 30 rue des Batignolles. Tel. 01/44.69.04.57. Open daily. *Info: 9th/Métro Saint-Georges or Pigalle. 48 rue Notre-Dame de Lorette. Tel. 01/53.21.90.17. Closed Mon. www.levinentete.fr.*

10ᵀᴴ Arrondissement
Gare du Nord/Canal St-Martin

The 10ᵗʰ arrondissement is home to two great train stations, the Gare du Nord and Gare de l'Est. It wasn't too long ago that guidebooks didn't even mention the 10th. Today, this working-class area is increasingly popular with artists, making for an interesting mix. Boutiques, cafés, galleries and trendy restaurants seem to have multiplied overnight.

SIGHTS

Winding through the 10th arrondissement on Paris's northeast side is the beautiful **Canal St-Martin**. The canal's bridges, footbridges and locks have been renovated. It's a great place to walk and relax.

RESTAURANTS & WINE BARS
Albion

This wine shop/bistro, located in the gentrifying 10th, not far from Gare du Nord and Gare de l'Est, is run by English chef Matthew Ong and New Zealand *sommelière* Hayden Clout. You'll find dark plank floors and walls lined with wine bottles. Servers are efficient (and if you don't speak French, you'll be just fine). Inventive, limited, menu and interesting wine list. Worth the trip. *Info: 10th/Métro Poissonière . 80 rue du Faubourg Poissonière (at rue des Messageries). Tel. 01/42.46.02.44. Closed Sat (lunch), Sun and Mon. www. restaurantalbion.com. Moderate.*

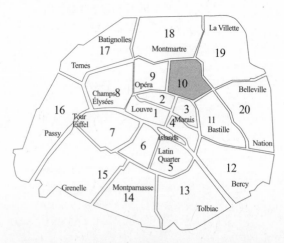

Vivant Table

Swiss-born Pierre Jancou has opened this casual wine bar/bistro in a color-fully tiled small shop that once sold exotic birds. You'll find Italian-Franco home-cooking in a funky neighborhood. Try the grilled *poularde* with organic vegetables. Excellent *foie gras* with *bortsch de betteraves* (beet soup). Selection of organic wines. *Info: 10th/Métro Bonne Nouvelle, Poissonière or Château d'Eau. 43 rue des Petites Ecuries (between rue du Faubourg Poissonière and rue d'Hauteville). Tel. 01/42.46.43.55. Closed Sat and Sun. www.vivantparis.com. Moderate.*

Brasserie Flo *Historic Restaurant*

Alsatian food and Parisian atmosphere at this 1886 brasserie, on a passageway in an area not frequented by tourists. Jam-packed with some of the strangest people you'll see in Paris, and getting there is half the fun. Try the *gigot d'agneau* (leg of lamb). *Info: 10th/Métro Château d'Eau. 7 cour des Petites-Écuries (enter from 63 rue du Fg-St-Denis). Tel. 01/47.70.13.59. Open daily until midnight. www.floparis.com. Expensive.*

Terminus Nord

What a great way to arrive in (or depart from) Paris! This large, bustling brasserie near the Gare du Nord is just so Parisian with its mahogany bar, polished wood and beveled glass. Seafood platters, *bouillabaisse* and duck breast are the featured dishes. *Info: 10th/Métro Gare du Nord. 23 rue de Dunkerque. Tel. 01/42.85.05.15. Open daily until midnight. www.terminusnord.com. Expensive.*

WINE SHOPS
Julhès

This *traiteur* (delicatessen/take-out) stocks a large selection of wine, including champagnes and many organic wines; and there's an excellent cheese department. In addition to its wines, it is also known for its spirits (especially whiskeys). *Info: 10th/ Métro Château d'Eau. 59 rue Faubourg Saint-Denis. Tel. 01/44.83.96.30. Open Mon 4pm-8:30pm. Tue-Sat 9:30am-8:30pm, Sun 9:30am-1:30pm. www.julhesparis.com.*

Le Verre Volé

This incredibly popular wine shop also has a small kitchen that turns out French comfort food. Excellent *charcuterie, pâtés*, and main courses from the chalkboard menu. You'll want to book ahead if you plan to eat here. Large selection of interesting wines by the glass. They also have a wine shop (that

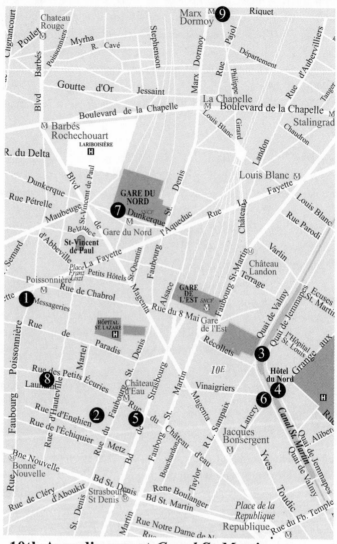

10th Arondissement *Canal St-Martin*

1. Albion
2. Brasserie Flo/
   Passage Brady
3. Canal St-Martin
4. Hôtel du Nord
5. Julhès
6. Le Verre Volé
7. Terminus Nord
8. Vivant Table
9. En Vrac

does not serve food) at 38 rue Oberkampf. Tel. 01/43.14.99.46. *Info: 10ᵗʰ/ Métro Jacques Bonsergent. 67 rue de Lancy. Tel. 01/48.03.17.34. Open daily. www.leverrevole.fr.*

DRINKING

The **zinc bar** at the 19th-century **Hôtel du Nord** is a great place to take a break. *Info: 10th/Métro J. Bonsergent or République. 102 quai de Jemmapes. Tel. 01/40.40.78.78. Café open daily 9am-1:30pm, restaurant open daily noon-3pm and 8pm-midnight.*

PASSAGE BRADY

Uniquely Parisian is *not* the **Passage Brady** in the 10th arrondissement. You can enter the narrow passage around 33 boulevard Strasbourg and find mostly Indian, but also Turkish and Moroccan, restaurants in an interesting setting. These are inexpensive restaurants in a working-class neighborhood, and the passage, while exotic in many ways, is not upscale (*Métro Château d'Eau*).

11ᵀᴴ ARRONDISSEMENT
Bastille

The 11th, centered on the Bastille, is primarily a residential area that has become increasingly hip lately, especially around rue de Charonne and rue de Lappe. Great restaurants!

SIGHTS
Opéra Bastille

Opened in 1989, this modern glass building hosts opera and symphony performances. *Info: 11th/Métro Bastille. East end of rue St-Antoine. Advanced reservations at www.operadeparis.fr (in English) or by calling from the U.S. 33.1.71.25.24.23.*

RESTAURANTS & WINE BARS
Chardenoux

This small, beautiful bistro has been in business for almost 100 years. Cyril Lignac, of television cooking-show fame, has taken over and updated its menu (and prices). The weekday prix fixe lunch at less than 30 euros lets you sample such dishes as *penne aux coquillages et chipirons, crème basilic* (penne with shellfish and squid in a basil cream sauce). *Info: 11th/Métro Charonne. 1 rue Jules-Vallès and 23 rue Chanzy. Tel. 01/43.71.49.52. Open daily. www. restaurantlechardenoux.com. Moderate-Expensive.*

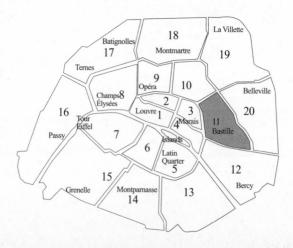

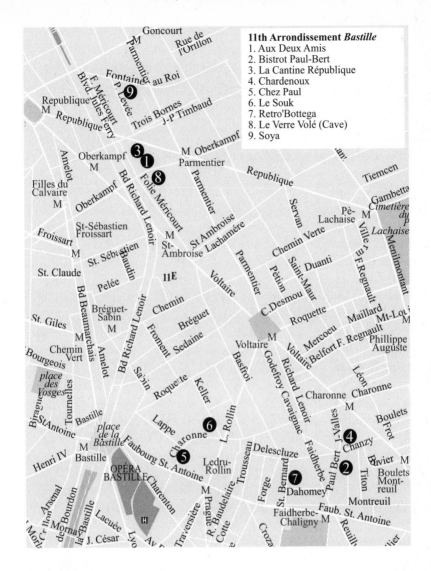

11th Arrondissement *Bastille*
1. Aux Deux Amis
2. Bistrot Paul-Bert
3. La Cantine République
4. Chardenoux
5. Chez Paul
6. Le Souk
7. Retro'Bottega
8. Le Verre Volé (Cave)
9. Soya

Bistrot Paul-Bert

A truly neighborhood bistro experience from its traditional decor to its menu written on a blackboard. Extensive wine list. Try the *entrecôte* (rib-eye steak) and the delicious *soufflé au chocolat*. <u>*Info:*</u> *11th/Métro Faidherbe-Chaligny. 18 rue Paul-Bert (near rue Chanzy). Tel. 01/43.72.24.01. Closed Sun, Mon and Aug. Moderate.*

Chez Paul

A favorite bistro in Paris. Never a bad meal, and ask to eat upstairs. The service can be very "Parisian." Try the *lapin* (rabbit). *Info: 11th/Métro Bastille or Ledru-Rollin. 13 rue de Charonne (at rue de Lappe). Tel. 01/47.00.34.57. Open daily. www.chezpaul.com. Moderate.*

Le Souk

This popular Moroccan restaurant with a good selection of vegetarian dishes is always busy and the interior is exotic. *Info: 11th/Métro Bastille or Ledru-Rollin. 1 rue Keller (near rue Charonne). Tel. 01/49.29.05.08. Closed Mon. No lunch Tue - Fri. www.lesoukfr.com. Moderate.*

Retro'Bottega

A little bit of Italy in Paris located on a small street in the 11th. This small (only four tables) Italian *épicerie* serves homemade Italian food. You'll eat surrounded by shelves brimming with wine, olive oil, and Italian specialties. Good selection of well-priced Italian and French wines *Info: 11th/Métro Faidherbe-Chaligny. 12 rue Saint-Bernard (off of rue de Faubourg Saint-Antoine. Tel. 01/74.64.17.39. Open Tue-Sat 10am-11pm. Closed Sun and Mon. Moderate.*

La Cantine République

Modern French cuisine at this no-frills spot near the place de la République. Try the *steak frites* (steak and French fries) or the *daurade au miel* (white fish, found in the South of France, in a honey sauce). The glassed-in sidewalk terrace allows you to take in some great people-watching. *Info: 11th/Métro Parmentier. 32 avenue de la République. Tel. 09/53.33.56.06. Open daily. Sunday brunch. www.lescantines.com. Inexpensive-Moderate.*

Aux Deux Amis

This wine bar in the Oberkampf area of the 11th has a copper-topped bar and mirrored walls. A crowd of locals and trend-setters sample small plates. Known for its market-based cooking and selection of organic wines by the glass. *Info: 11th/Métro Oberkampf. 45 rue Oberkampf. Tel. 01/58.30.38.13. Closed Sun and Mon. Moderate.*

Fermé la Dimanche

Closed on Sunday.

Soya

You'll find inventive vegetarian dishes at this small, intimate restaurant. Try the lasagna stuffed with tofu. Excellent list of organic wines. *Info: 11th/ Métro République. 20 rue de la Pierre Levée (off of rue de la Fontaine-au-Roi). Tel. 01/48.06.33.02. Closed Sat. (dinner) and Sun. (dinner). www.soya75. fr. Moderate*

WINE SHOP
Le Verre Volé (Cave)

Le Verre Volé is an incredibly popular wine shop specializing in organic wines. Its main location (which also features a small kitchen) is located in the 10th at 67 rue de Lancy. Tel. 01/48.03.17.34. *Info: 11th/Métro Oberkampf. 38 rue Oberkampf. Tel. 01/43.14.99.46. Open daily. www.leverrevole.fr.*

12ᵀᴴ & 13ᵀᴴ Arrondissements
Gare de Lyon/Bois de Vincennes
Place d'Italie

The 12th is home to the Gare de Lyon train station. This primarily residential area is bordered on the east by the Bois de Vincennes, a beautiful park. The 13th is a residential area, home to Place d'Italie, Chinatown (13 square blocks around the Tolbiac métro stop) and the grand National Library.

SIGHTS

Bibliothèque Nationale de France

France's National Library, the pet project of former president François Mitterand, has four towers that were designed to represent open books (it's a library, after all). It has a wonderful bookstore, and there's a peaceful sunken courtyard. If you're not a scholar, you'll probably just want to take a look at the immense exterior and down into the courtyard garden. *Info: 13th/Métro Bibliothèque. quai François-Mauriac. Tel. 01/53.79.59.59. Closed Sun and Mon morning. Admission: €3.50 (to reading rooms). www.bnf.fr.*

Bois de Vincennes

Past the medieval castle, **Château de Vincennes** (*Tel. 01/48.08.31.20, open daily 10am-5pm. Admission: €8.50, under 18 free*), is the Bois de Vincennes (woods) containing a beautiful floral park, the **Parc Floral**

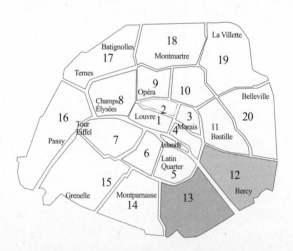

(Tel. 01/43.43.92.95, open daily. Admission: €5.50, under 7 free). If you're interested in gardening, especially flowers, you'll enjoy viewing not only the seasonal flowers, but also the bamboo, bonsai, medicinal plants and ferns (all labeled with their latin names). *Info: 12th/Métro Château de Vincennes. Eastern edge of Paris. www.parcfloraldeparis.com.*

RESTAURANTS & WINE BARS

Le Train Bleu Historic Restaurant
Forget all the food you've eaten in train stations. It's delicious here. The setting, with its murals of the French-speaking world, is spectacular. A great place to have a drink. *Info: 12th/Métro Gare-de-Lyon. 20 boulevard Diderot (in the Gare de Lyon train station). Tel. 01/43.43.09.06. Open daily until 11pm. www. le-train-bleu.com. Expensive.*

Aux Petit Marguery
This 1930s bistro features outstanding game dishes and is known for its *Grand Marnier soufflé* and good service. Good old-fashioned French cuisine. *Info:*

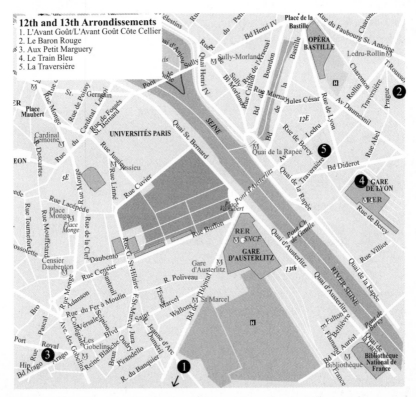

12th and 13th Arrondissements
1. L'Avant Goût/L'Avant Goût Côte Cellier
2. Le Baron Rouge
3. Aux Petit Marguery
4. Le Train Bleu
5. La Traversière

13th/Métro Les Gobelins. 9 boulevard de Port-Royal (near av. des Gobelins). Tel. 01/43.31.58.59. Open daily. www.petitmarguery.fr. Moderate.

L'Avant Goût

Mix with the French in this small, crowded bistro near the place d'Italie. Consistently good cuisine and very French. Try the *pot-au-feu* (stew of meat and vegetables). *Info: 13th/Métro Place d'Italie. 26 rue Bobillot (from place d'Italie, south on rue Bobillot). Tel. 01/53.80.24.00. Closed Sun, Mon and most of Aug. www.lavantgout.com. Moderate.*

Le Traversière

This restaurant is off the beaten track where you'll be dining with locals on traditional French cuisine. A solid choice if you're in the area. Basic décor and friendly service. The restaurant frequently features game dishes. Try *le filet de boeuf aux morilles* (beef fillet with morel mushrooms) when available. The *homard* (lobster) is also a good choice. *Info: 12ᵗʰ/Metro Ledru-Rollin. 40 rue Traversière. Tel. 01/43.44.02.10. Closed Sun and Mon. Moderate-Expensive.*

Le Baron Rouge

Have a glass of wine (some right from the barrel) at this neighborhood wine bar. You'll sit at communal tables. Try the *charcuterie*, cheese platters, and

 oysters (on weekends). It's especially busy on Sunday afternoons. *Info: 12ᵗʰ/Métro Ledru-Rollin. 1 rue Théophile Roussel. Tel. 01/43.43.14.32. Closed Sun (dinner) and Mon. Moderate.*

WINE SHOPS
Les Crus du Soleil

This wine shop (with a devoted following) specializes in wines and products from the Languedoc-Roussillon region in the South of France. There's a small area for wine tastings. *Info: 12ᵗʰ/Métro Ledru-Rollin. 21 rue d'Aligre. Tel. 01/43.43.52.20. Open Tue-Fri 10am-1pm and 3:30pm-8:30pm, Sat 10am-8:30pm, Sun 10am-1pm. www.crus-du-soleil.com. There's also a shop in the 14ᵗʰ/Métro Pernety. 146 rue du Château. Tel. 01/45.39.78.99.*

L'Avant Goût Côté Cellier
The bistro L'Avant Goût (see above) operates this small wine shop specializing in wines from small French producers. It's on the same block as the bistro. *Info: 13ᵗʰ/Métro Place d'Italie. 37 rue Bobillot. Tel. 01/45.81.14.06. Open Tue-Fri, 10am-3pm and 5pm-8pm, Sat, 10am-1pm and 3pm-8pm. Closed Sun and Mon.*

14ᵀᴴ & 15ᵀᴴ ARRONDISSEMENTS
Montparnasse

Known as Montparnasse and centered around the lively boulevard Montparnasse (once the center of Paris's avant-garde scene), these areas are primarily residential.

SIGHTS
Cimetière du Montparnasse

This quiet but somewhat messy cemetery is the "permanent home" of Samuel Beckett, Jean-Paul Sartre, Simone de Beauvoir and other celebrities of the past. *Info: 14th/Métro Edgar Quinet. Enter on either rue Froidevaux or boulevard Edgar Quinet off of boulevard Raspail. Open daily 9am-5:30pm. Admission: Free.*

Fondation Cartier

This contemporary art-and-photography museum is housed in an incredible glass building. *Info: 14th/Métro Raspail. 261 boulevard Raspail. Tel. 01/42.18.56.50. Open Tue-Sun 11am-8pm (Tue until 10pm). Closed Mon. Admission: €9.50, under 10 free. www.fondation.cartier.com.*

Les Catacombes

Grim, strange and claustrophobic. Beginning in the late 1700s, six million people were deposited in what used to be stone quarries. It gets even creepier.

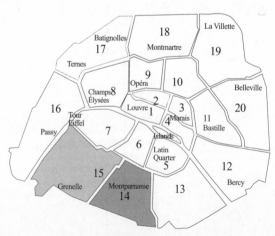

The bones are arranged in patterns. Not for everyone. *Info: 14th/Métro Denfert-Rochereau. 1 place Denfert-Rochereau. Tel. 01/43.22.47.63. Open Tue-Sun 10am-5pm. Closed Mon. Admission: €8, under 13 free.*

Musée du Quai Branly

At its fabulous site along the Seine near the Eiffel Tower, this new museum is dedicated to the arts and civilizations of Africa, Asia, Oceania and the Americas. One of the walls of the museum, along Quai Branly, is completely covered with plants cascading down the walls. You have to see it. Even if you don't tour the museum, you should definitely visit the free garden. The garden café here is a good place to take a break. *Info: 15th/Métro École Militaire or Bir-Hakeim. 37 bis Quai Branly. Tel. 01/56.61.70.00. Open Tue-Sun 11am-7pm (Thu, Fri and Sat until 9pm). Closed Mon, May 1 and Dec 25. Admission: €8.50, under 18 free. Free on the first Sun of each month. www.quaibranly.fr.*

Tour Montparnasse (Montparnasse Tower)

This unfortunate 1970s black glass tower that dominates its Left Bank neighbors has an observation deck. Take the elevator to the 56th floor and then steps to the roof. There was such outrage after this tower was built that an ordinance was passed prohibiting further towers in the city center. The best thing about the great view is that you can't see this tower! *Info: 15th/ Métro Montparnasse-Bienvenüe. Open daily Apr-Sep 9:30am-11:30pm, Oct-Mar 9:30am-10:30pm. Last ascension a half-hour before closing. Admission: €13.50, under 7 free.*

Musée de la Poste

The Postal Museum is devoted to French and international philately (stamp collections). *Info: 15th/Métro Pasteur or Montparnasse-Bienvenüe. 34 boulevard de Vaugirard. Tel. 01/42.79.24.24. Open Mon-Sat 10am-6pm. Closed Sun. Admission: €5, under 13 free. www.museedelaposte.fr.*

Musée Bourdelle

Bourdelle was a student of Rodin. Bourdelle's famous 21 studies of Beethoven are housed here. *Info: 15th/Métro Montparnasse-Bienvenüe or Falguière. 16-18 rue Antoine Bourdelle. Tel. 01/49.54.73.73. Open Tue-Sun 10am-6pm. Closed Mon. Admission: Permanent collection is free. €7 for exhibits.*

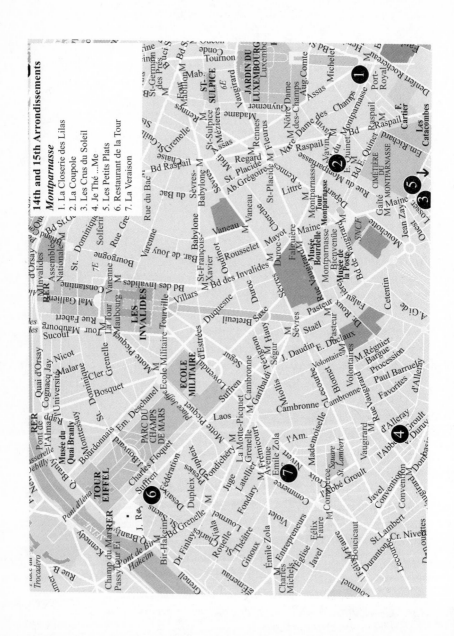

14th and 15th Arrondissements

Montparnasse

1. La Closerie des Lilas
2. La Coupole
3. Les Crus du Soleil
4. Je Thé ...Me
5. Les Petits Plats
6. Restaurant de la Tour
7. La Veraison

RESTAURANTS & WINE BARS

La Closerie des Lilas *Historic Restaurant*
Lenin and Trotsky are among those who have visited this historic café. There's a terrace, piano bar, brasserie (moderate) and restaurant (expensive). The brasserie is known for its *steak tartare*. *Info: 14th/Métro Raspail or Vavin. 171 boulevard du Montparnasse (near blvd. Saint-Michel). Tel. 01/40.51.34.50. Open daily. Moderate-Expensive.*

La Coupole *Historic Restaurant*
A Montparnasse institution since the days of Picasso, this noisy brasserie known for its *huîtres* (oysters) is a favorite among tourists. *Info: 14th/Métro Vavin. 102 boulevard du Montparnasse (at rue Vavin). Tel. 01/43.20.14.20. Open daily until midnight. www.lacoupoleparis.com. Expensive.*

Restaurant de la Tour
You'll be welcomed by the friendly owners to the lovely dining room with Provençal décor where you'll dine on classic French fare. Try the delicious *sanglier* (wild boar). After dinner, head to the brilliantly lit Eiffel Tower, just a few blocks away. *Info: 15th/Métro Dupleix. 6 rue Desaix (near av. de Suffren. Tel. 01/43.06.04.24. Closed Sat, Sun, and Aug. www.restaurant-delatour.fr. Moderate-Expensive.*

Je Thé ... Me
This attractive bistro in a century-old grocery store serves classic French fare. Friendly. Try the *potage du marché* (a thick soup). *Info: 15th/Métro Vaugirard. 4 rue d'Alleray (off of rue de Vaugirard). Tel. 01/48.42.48.30. Closed Sun, Mon and Aug. Moderate.*

La Veraison
This casual restaurant is a real find. You'll see the chef cooking as you walk in. The food is a modern take on traditional French cooking. And it's fun to go off the beaten path. Excellent veal, and don't miss the chocolate and creme caramel dessert. *Info: 15th/Métro Commerce. 64 rue de la Croix Nivert (at rue du Théâtre). Tel. 01/45.32.39.39. Closed Sat (lunch) and Sun. www.laveraison. com. Moderate.*

Les Petits Plats
This relaxed and friendly bistro is a good choice in the 14th arrondissement. All the selections on the blackboard menu are available in both full and half

portions. If you're here for dinner, try the tasting menu for about €37. The fixed price lunch is a good value at €17. When available, try the sautéed scallops and squid or tasty gazpacho. And if you're looking for a roomy table and a quiet dining experience, you'll need to go elsewhere! _Info: 14th/Métro Alésia. 39 rue des Plantes (off of rue d'Alésia). Tel. 01/45.42.50.52. Closed Sun and most of Aug. Moderate._

WINE SHOP
Les Crus du Soleil
This wine shop (with a devoted following) specializes in wines and products from the Languedoc-Roussillon region in the South of France. There's a small area for wine tastings. _Info: 14th/Métro Pernety. 146 rue du Château. Tel. 01/45.39.78.99. Open Tue-Fri 10am-1pm and 3:30pm-8:30pm, Sat 10am-8:30pm, Sun 10am-1pm.www.crus-du-soleil.com, There's also a shop in the 12th/Métro Ledru-Rollin. 21 rue d'Aligre. Tel. 01/43.43.52.20._

16ᵀᴴ & 17ᵀᴴ ARRONDISSEMENTS
Trocadéro/Arc de Triomphe
Parc Monceau/Place Clichy

You'll find upscale shopping, elegant residences and parks such as the Trocadéro in the 16th arrondissement. The Arc de Triomphe and beautiful Parc Monceau border the residential 17th.

SIGHTS

Across the river from the Eiffel Tower, the **Musée National des Arts Asiatiques–Guimet** houses a world-famous collection of Asian art. _Info: 16th/Métro Iéna. 6 place d'Iéna. Tel. 01/56.52.53.00. Open Wed-Mon 10am-6pm. Closed Tue., May 1, Dec 25, and Jan1. Admission: €7.50, €5.50 ages 18-25, under 18 free. www.guimet.fr._

If you're interested in more contemporary art, the **Musée d'Art Moderne de la Ville de Paris** houses the city's modern-art collection (including murals by Matisse), and hosts traveling exhibits. _Info: 16th/Métro Iéna. 11 avenue du Président Wilson. Tel. 01/53.67.40.00. Open noon-6pm Tue-Sun (until 10pm on Thu). Admission: Depends on exhibit._

The **Palais de Tokyo** is a contemporary art center in a colossal Art Nouveau building. _Info: 16th/Métro Iéna. 13 avenue du Président Wilson._

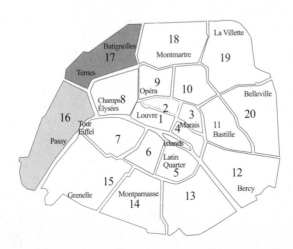

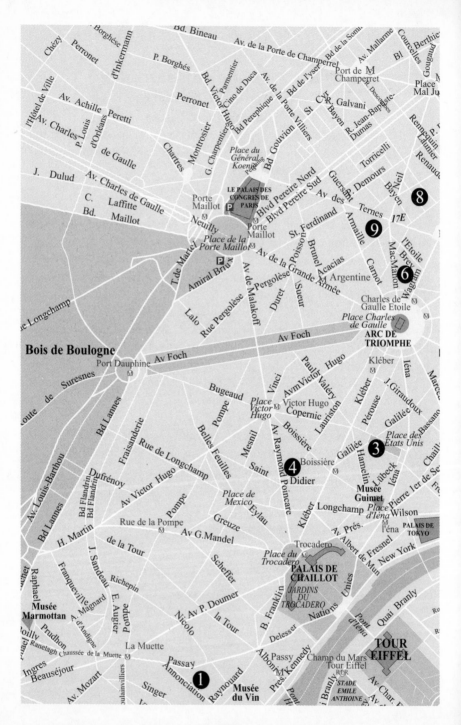

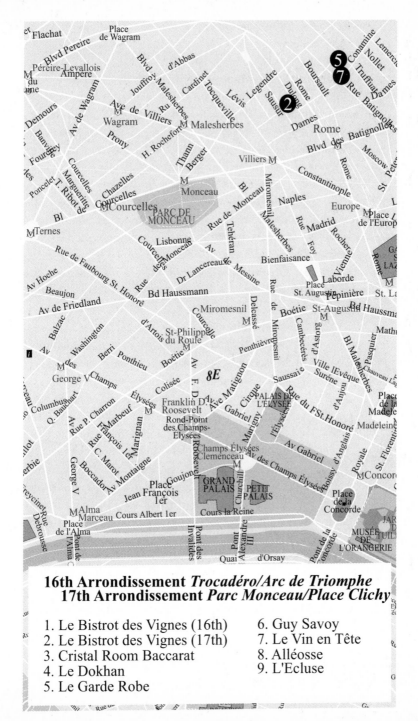

16th Arrondissement *Trocadéro/Arc de Triomphe*
17th Arrondissement *Parc Monceau/Place Clichy*

1. Le Bistrot des Vignes (16th)
2. Le Bistrot des Vignes (17th)
3. Cristal Room Baccarat
4. Le Dokhan
5. Le Garde Robe
6. Guy Savoy
7. Le Vin en Tête
8. Alléosse
9. L'Ecluse

Tel. 01/81.97.35.88. Open noon-midnight Tue-Sun. Admission: €10, under 18 free. www.palaisdetokyo.com.

Musée Marmottan-Claude Monet is named after Paul Marmottan, who donated his beautiful home to house his collection of historic furnishings. In 1966, when Monet's son died in an automobile accident, the museum received over 130 works by the artist, including *Impression-Sunrise*, from which the Impressionist movement is said to have gotten its name. In addition to the well-known water lilies and paintings of his house in Giverny, you'll also see Renoir's portrait of Monet. *Info: 16th/Métro La Muette. 2 rue Louis-Boilly. Tel. 01/44.96.50.33. Open 10am-6pm, Thurs until 8pm. Closed Mon. Admission: €10, €5 ages 8-18, under 8 free. From the métro stop, walk west on Chaussée de la Muette which turns into avenue du Ranelagh. Turn right onto avenue Raphaël. The museum is on the corner of avenue Raphaël and rue Louis-Boilly. The walk from the métro stop to the museum is a half mile. www.marmottan.com.*

Where else can you enjoy a glass of wine while discovering the noble art of wine-making? The **Musée du Vin** (Wine Museum) is dedicated to France's winemaking heritage. Exhibits of tools and memorabilia allow you to discover its traditions. It's located in ancient vaults and cellars dating back to the Middle Ages. Oh, and admission includes one glass of wine! *Info: 16th/Métro Passy. 5 square Charles Dickens off of the rue des Eaux. Tel. 01/45.25.63.26. Open Tue-Sun 10am-6pm. Closed Mon. Admission: €12. www.museeduvinparis.com.*

Bois de Boulogne

An enormous park (nearly 2,200 acres) open 24 hours a day (avoid it at night). Walking paths, lakes, a waterfall, an amusement park (see above), children's zoo and two horse racetracks are all here. **Parc de St-Cloud** is another less-crowded park at the western end of métro line 10 (Métro Boulogne/Pont de St-Cloud). Come here for fountains, flowers, ponds and tranquil walks. *Info: On the western edge of the 16th/Métro Porte Dauphine.* The **Jardin d'Acclimatation** is located in the northern 25 acres of the Bois de Boulogne. Take a ride on Le Petit Train (small train) to the amusement park entrance from the Porte Maillot métro stop, which departs every 30 minutes (€3). Playgrounds, pony rides, a zoo, miniature golf course, bowling alleys, a hall of mirrors … you get the picture. There are several restaurants and cafés in the park. *Info: 16th/Métro Porte Maillot or Les Sablons. Tel. 01/40.67.90.85. Open daily May-Sep 10am-7pm (Oct-Apr until 6pm). Admission: €3, under 3 free. www.jardindacclimatation.fr.*

RESTAURANTS & WINE BARS
Cristal Room Baccarat
This elegant restaurant is owned by the Baccarat crystal company. The boutique and museum are located across the street. The setting is appropriate, a 1900 stone mansion, with dozens of crystal chandeliers (all for sale for over $100,000, in case you're interested). *Info: 16th/Métro Boissière. place des Etats-Unis. Tel. 01/40.22.11.10. Closed Sun. Reservations required. Expensive.*

Le Garde Robe
This wine bar in the residential 17th features mostly organic wines (with an emphasis on white wines from Loire) and has a knowledgeable staff. Delicious *charcuterie* and cheese plates. Its other location is in the 1st at 41 rue de l'Arbre Sec. *Info: 17th/Métro Rome or La Fourche. 4 rue Bridaine. Tel. 01/44.90.05.04. Open daily. Moderate.*

Guy Savoy
Guy Savoy is one of France's top chefs. Start with a bowl of artichoke soup topped with shavings of aged Parmesan and served with a truffle-buttered *brioche* (it's the restaurant's signature dish). The chef is frequently present and may greet you at your table. An incredible and very expensive dining experience. Known for its extensive wine list. *Info: 17th/Métro Charles-de-Gaulle-Étoile or Ternes. 18 rue Troyon. Tel. 01/43.80.40.61. Reservations required. www.guysavoy.com. Very Expensive.*

Le Bistrot des Vignes
Looking for a place to dine on a Sunday? This may just be your choice. There are two locations (one in the 16th and one in the 17th). You'll have a warm welcome and dine in a comfortable and contemporary setting. Start with the *foie gras de canard maison, chutney d'ananas* (duck foie gras with pineapple chutney). For a main course, try *travers de porc laqué au miel et gingembre* (pork ribs glazed with honey and ginger) or *sauté d'agneau au cumin et à la coriandre* (sautéed lamb with cumin and coriander). Very reasonable €17

weekday fixed-priced lunch. Brunch is served on the weekends. *Info: 16th/ Métro La Muette or Passy. 1 rue Jean Bologne. Tel. 01/45.27.76.64. Open daily for lunch and dinner. Also 17th/Métro Rome or Villiers. 90 rue des Dames. www. bistrotdesvignes.fr.*

L'Ecluse
Chain of wine bars. Not the greatest food in Paris, but good for wine tasting (especially Bordeaux). Decent selection of wines by the glass and light meals such as *charcuterie assortie* (assorted cold meats). This location has a large wine shop. *Info: 17th/Métro Charles de Gaulle - Etoile. 1 rue d'Armaillé (at avenue Carnot). Tel. 01/47.63.88.29. Open daily with continuous service from 8:30am to 1am. www.leclusebaravin.com.*

Other locations include:
• 15 quai des Grands Augustins (6th/Métro St-Michel)
• 64 rue François 1er (Métro 8th/Métro George V)
• 15 place de la Madeleine (8th/Métro Madeleine)
• 34 place du Marché Saint Honoré (1st/Métro Louvre, Tuileries or Pyramides)

WINE SHOP
Le Vin en Tête
This wine shop offers wines from all of France's regions and a selection of foreign wines, and specializes in organic wines. *Info: 17th/Métro Rome or Place du Clichy. 30 rue des Batignolles. Tel. 01/44.69.04.57. Open daily. www. levinentete.fr. You can also visit them in the 9th/Métro Saint-Georges or Pigalle. 48 rue Notre-Dame de Lorette. Tel. 01/53.21.90.17. Closed Mon.*

DRINKING
Le Dokhan
Before (or after) dinner, you might want to have a glass of champagne. Le Dokhan (located in Trocadéro Dokhan's Hôtel) is an elegant champagne bar where you can enjoy it by the flute or by the bottle. *Info: 16th/Métro Trocadéro. 117 rue Lauriston. Tel. 01/53.65.66.99. Open daily (evenings only).*

CHEESE SHOP
Alléosse
Cheese is like gold to the French. Charles de Gaulle is reported to have said, "How can anyone govern a nation that has 246 different kinds of cheese?" This pretty cheese shop serves rare cheeses from throughout France. It's

located on a busy market street. *Info: 17th/Métro Ternes. 13 rue Poncelet. Tel. 01/46.22.50.45. Closed Sun (afternoon) and Mon.*

WORLD"S BIGGEST WINE TASTING

Several times a year, the **Vigneron Independent** (a trade association of independent winemakers) sponsors wine tastings. For only €6 euro you can taste as many wines as you want from independent producers from all over France, and you can also buy direct from the winemakers if you like anything. You see people hauling home cases on the métro. The fall salon is usually held at the Porte de Versailles in the 15th arrondissment. The spring salon is usually at the Espace Champerret at the Parc d'exposition in the 17th arrondissement. Check out *www.vigneron-independant.com/auxsalons/* (in French) if you're interested.

18ᵀᴴ ARRONDISSEMENT
Montmartre

Once a small village of vineyards and windmills, Montmartre is dominated by the massive Sacred Heart Basilica. It's also home to the sleazy place Pigalle and the largest flea market in Paris.

SIGHTS
Basilique du Sacré-Coeur

The Sacred Heart Basilica is located at the top of the hill (*butte*) in Montmartre. It's named for Christ's heart, which some believe is in the crypt. You can't miss it, with its white onion domes and Byzantine and Romanesque architecture. Inside you'll find gold mosaics, but the real treat is the view of Paris from the dome or the square directly in front of the basilica. *Info: 18ᵗʰ/Métro Anvers or Abbesses. place Parvis-du-Sacré-Coeur. Tel. 01/53.41.89.00. Open daily 6am-10:30pm. Observation deck and crypt 9am-7pm (until 6pm in winter). Admission: Free. To the observation deck in the dome and to the crypt is €5. www.sacre-coeur-montmartre.com.*

Espace Salvador-Dali

Black walls, weird music with Dali's voice and dim lighting all make this place an interesting experience. Come here if you're a fan of Salvador Dali to see 300 of his lithographs and etchings and 25 sculptures. *Info: 18th/ Métro Abbesses. 11 rue Poulbot. Tel. 01.42.64.40.10. Open daily 10am-6pm*

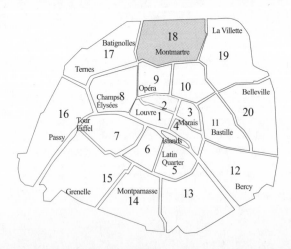

(until 8pm Jul and Aug). Admission: €11, 6 ages 8-26, under 8 free. www. daliparis.com.

Musée du Vieux Montmartre
Renoir and van Gogh are just a few of the artists who have occupied this 17th-century house. It's now a museum with a collection of mementos of this neighborhood, including paintings, posters and photographs. *Info: 18th/ Métro Anvers. 12 rue Cortot. Tel. 01/49.25.89.37. Open daily 10am-6pm. Admission: €8, under 10 free. www.museedemontmartre.fr.*

Moulin Rouge
You've seen the movie, now see the cancan. Originally a red windmill, the Moulin Rouge dance hall has been around since 1889. It's without a doubt the most famous cabaret in the world. Toulouse-Lautrec memorialized the Moulin Rouge in his paintings. Looking for a little bit of Vegas? You'll find it here. *Info: 18th/Métro Blanche. 82 boulevard de Clichy. Tel. 01/53.09.82.82. Shows nightly at 9pm and 11pm. Admission: €105 (11pm show with half bottle of champagne). €175-200 (7pm dinner followed by 9pm show). www. moulinrouge.fr.*

place Pigalle
If you're really a late-night, adventurous type, you can head to the sleazy place Pigalle. You come here for only one thing: sex. Littered with sex shops, this area was known as "Pig Alley" during World War II. During the day, neighborhood residents walking with their children and eating ice cream seem oblivious to all the sex shops, reminding us that this is, after all, just another Paris neighborhood. *Info: 18th/Métro Pigalle. Eastern end of boulevard de Clichy.*

While here, you can visit yet another museum (of a different sort). The **Musée de l'Erotisme** (Museum of Erotic Art) is devoted to erotic art. 2,000 paintings, photos, carvings (can you say "dildo"?), implements ... Well, you get the picture. Not surprisingly, the museum remains open until the wee hours of the morning. There's also a "gift" shop, of course. *Info: 18th/Métro Blanche. 72 blvd. de Clichy. Tel. 01.42.58.28.73. Open daily 10am-2am. Admission: €8. www.musee-erotisme.com.*

Clignancourt Flea Market
This is the **Marché aux Puces** ("flea market"), the most famous in Paris. When you get off at the métro stop, just follow the crowds. Work your way through the junk on the outskirts of the market (watch your wallet) until you find the interesting antique dealers around rue des Rosiers and avenue Michelet. You can find all sorts of small souvenirs to take home. If you get hungry, there are cheap snack stands and a few good restaurants. *Info: 18th/ Métro Porte de Clignancourt (cross boulevard Ney). Open Sat-Mon 9am-6pm.*

RESTAURANTS & WINE BARS
Le Grand 8
This friendly, small bistro is located in Montmartre near Sacrè-Coeur. Unlike most places in this touristy area, most diners are from the neighborhood. Start with a *salade de chèvre chaud* (warm goat cheese salad) and dine on such main courses as *carré d'agneau accompagné d'un gratin de pommes de terre* (rack of lamb with potato gratin) or *filets de pigeon, purée carottes* (pigeon with a carrot purée). Interesting selection of wines by the glass and bottle. Ask for a seat near the back window and enjoy the great view. *Info: 18th/Métro Lamarck-Caulaincourt. 8 rue Lamarck. Tel. 01/42.55.04.55. Closed Mon. No lunch except Sat and Sun. www.legrand8.fr. Moderate.*

Bar-tabac des Deux Moulins
The movie *Amélie* won not only many film awards, but also a cult following. The lead character is a waitress. Here you can visit Amélie's 1950s bistro, where you'll find mostly locals enjoying good homemade desserts and standard bistro fare. *Info: 18th/Métro Blanche. 15 rue Lepic. Tel. 01/42.54.90.50. Open daily. Moderate.*

La Cave des Abbesses
A great place to stop before or after you get off the metro at Abbesses for your visit to Montmartre. There's a decent selection of estate-bottled wines at the wine shop. You can buy a bottle and drink it with *charcuterie* and cheese platters offered in the back of the shop. *Info: 18th/Métro Abbesses. 43 rue des Abbesses. Open Tue-Fri evenings, Sat and Sun noon-9:30pm. Tel. 01/42.52.81.54. Moderate.*

Le Bal Cafe
This café/exhibition space is a favorite. Hours are a little inconvenient for the traveler, as dinner is only served on Thursdays: It's a good place to hang

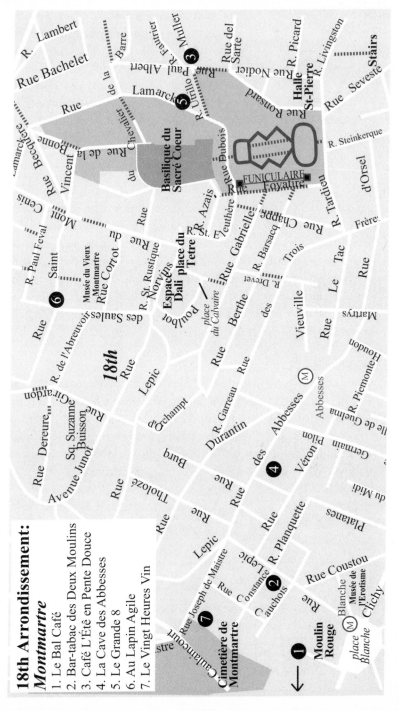

18th Arrondissement:
Montmartre

1. Le Bal Café
2. Bar-tabac des Deux Moulins
3. Café L'Été en Pente Douce
4. La Cave des Abbesses
5. Le Grande 8
6. Au Lapin Agile
7. Le Vingt Heures Vin

out outside dining hours. Tea, coffee, hot chocolate, hot ginger beer, great wine selection, and delicious desserts. The staff speaks excellent English. *Info: 18th/Métro Clichy. 6 impasse de la Défense (a short walk north from the place de Clichy on avenue de Clichy. On the ight side of the street between rue Capron and rue Ganneron). Tel. 01/44.70.75.51. Closed Mon and Tue. Lunch Wed through Fri, Brunch Sat and Sun, Dinner Thu only. www.le-bal.fr. Moderate.*

En Vrac

The name means "in bulk" and you can have bottles (with stoppers) filled with your choice of wines to go. At €4 to €8 a bottle, that's quite a deal. The bar is lined with wine-filled steel tanks. There's a *plat du jour* along with cheese plates, *charcuterie*, and sandwiches made to order. They also offer classes where you can learn to make your own wine. *Info: 18th/Métro Marx Dormoy. 2 rue de l'Olive (at the corner of 92 rue Riquet). Tel. 01/53.26.03.94. Open daily 10am-midnight.www.vinenvrac.fr/en. Inexpensive. See 10th Arrondissement Map on page 80.*

Le Vingt Heures Vin

The owner of this vibrant wine bar in Montmartre (there's another location in the 11th) is a wine buff who'll help you with your selection. Relax over a glass or bottle of wine with bread, cheese, *charcuterie*, small plates, or a salad (the "Emile Buisson" vegetarian salad is a good choice). Try *la tartine chic* with ham, tomato, basil, and cheese. Popular late at night. *Info: 18th/ Métro Abbesses. 15/17 rue Joseph de Maistre. Tel. 09/54.66.50.67. Open Tue-Sun 7pm to 1am. Also at 11th/Métro Goncourt. 2 rue des Goncourt (off of rue Parmentier near place de la République). Tel. 01/49.29.79.56. Open Tue-Sat at 6pm. Sunday brunch from noon to 2pm. www.vingtheuresvin.com.*

CAFE BREAK NEAR THE BASILICA

The **Café L'Été en Pente Douce** is an interesting and picturesque café near Sacré-Coeur. Take a break here before you climb the steps to the basilica! *Info: 18th/Métro Château-Rouge. 23 rue Muller. Tel. 01/42.64.02.67. Open daily 7:30am to 1am. Moderate.*

DRINKING
Au Lapin Agile

You'll hear French folk tunes at this shuttered cottage at the picturesque intersection of rue des Saules and rue St-Vincent. It was once frequented by Picasso. You'll sit at small wooden tables and listen to *chansonniers* (singers). Truly a Parisian experience. *Info: 18th/Métro Lamarck-Caulaincourt. Intersection of rue des Saules and rue St-Vincent. Tel. 01/46.06.85.87. Open Tue-Sun 9pm-2am. Closed Mon. Admission: €24 (includes a drink). No credit cards. Reservations can be made at www.au-lapin-agile.com.*

19ᵀᴴ & 20ᵀᴴ Arrondissements
Parc de La Villette
Père-Lachaise Cemetery

Many visitors to Paris ignore areas of the city that are easily accessible, but a little off the beaten path. The diverse residential areas of the 19th and 20th arrondissements are home to the Parc de la Villette and the Cimetière du Père-Lachaise.

SIGHTS

The futuristic **Parc de La Villette** is more than just a park. It features gardens and paths, but also has modern sculptures and bizarre park benches. A great place for kids. For years, this was the site of the city's slaughterhouses. *Info: 19th/ Métro Porte de Pantin.*

Musée de la Musique

Located in the Cité de la Musique (the $120 million stone-and-glass part of the Parc de la Villette), this museum features over 4,000 musical instruments from Baroque Italy to present-day France. You'll be given a headset (available in English). As you stroll through the museum, every time you approach an exhibit, the headset begins to play the music of that instrument. Very entertaining for kids and adults. *Info: 19th/ Métro Porte de Pantin. 221 avenue Jean-Jaurès. Tel. 01/44.84.45.00. Open Tue-Sat noon-6pm, Sun 10am-6pm. Closed Mon. Admission: €8, under 26 free. www.cite-musique.fr.*

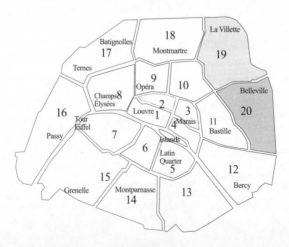

Cité des Sciences et de l'Industrie (City of Science and Industry)
This huge and spectacular museum is dedicated to science and industry, including **La Géode** (geodesic dome), a planetarium, aquarium, a submarine and much more. _Info: 19th/Métro Porte de La Villette. At the northern edge of the city in the Parc de La Villette. 30 avenue Corentine-Cariou. Tel. 01/40.05.70.00. Open Tue-Sat 9:30am-6pm, Sun 10am-7pm. Closed Mon. Admission: €11, €9 ages 6-25, under 6 free. www.cite-sciences.fr._

Parc des Buttes-Chaumont
Created in 1867 (from a former garbage dump), this peaceful park has artificial cliffs, streams, waterfalls and jogging paths. _Info: 19th/Métro Botzaris. rue Manin. Open daily 7am-sunset. Admission: Free._

Cimetière du Père-Lachaise
In 1626, the Jesuits opened a retreat for retired priests on this site. Father (_Père_) Lachaise, Louis XIV's confessor, visited here often. The Jesuits were expelled in 1763 and the city bought the property (all 110 acres) and converted it into a cemetery. It's the largest cemetery in Paris and is the eternal home to an incredible list of people, including Maria Callas, Chopin, Oscar Wilde, Balzac, Bellini, Proust, Modigliani, Gertrude Stein and Edith Piaf. Oh yeah, Jim Morrison of _The Doors_ is buried here, too (you will see hordes of fans near his grave, a pilgrimage site for his admirers). The graves range from simple, unadorned headstones to elaborate monuments and chapels.

The grounds are quite beautiful and there are over 3,000 trees here. Each family is responsible for the upkeep of the family plot, and some are in extreme states of disrepair. There's a new 30-year-lease policy in place, so if the family doesn't renew the lease, the remains can be removed. It's believed that Jim Morrison's lease will never expire, much to the dismay of families who have their plots nearby.

If you enter the cemetery from the back off of rue des Rondeaux, you'll find the **Jardin du Souvenir**, with a series of stark, heart-wrenching memorials and tombstones dedicated to those who died in military combat or concentration camps during World War II. _Info: 20th/Métro Père-Lachaise. Enter off the boulevard de Ménilmontant. Open daily Mon-Fri 8am-6pm, Sat 8:30am-6pm, Sun and holidays 9am-6pm. Closes at 5:30pm Nov-early Mar. Free maps available at the main entrance when a guard is on duty. Admission: Free. www.pere-lachaise.com._

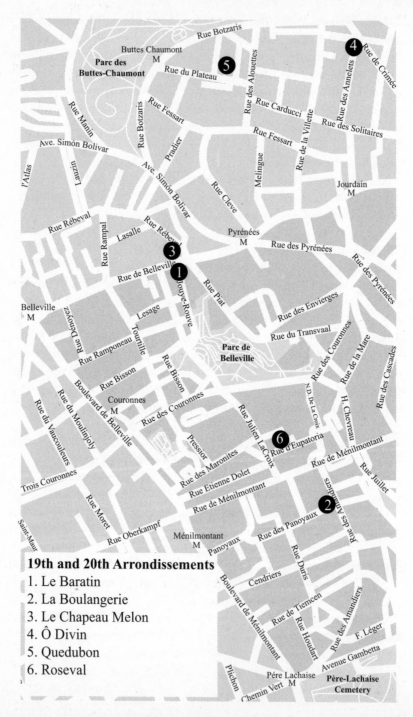

19th and 20th Arrondissements
1. Le Baratin
2. La Boulangerie
3. Le Chapeau Melon
4. Ô Divin
5. Quedubon
6. Roseval

RESTAURANTS, WINE BARS & WINE SHOPS

La Boulangerie

Classic French bistro with a mosaic floor in a former bakery near Père-Lachaise cemetery. Good selection of wines by the glass. Try the excellent *carré d'agneau en croûte de moutarde et herbes* (rack of lamb encrusted with mustard and herbs). *Info: 20th/Métro Ménilmontant. 15 rue des Panoyaux (off of blvd. de Ménilmontant). Tel. 01/43.58.45.45. Closed Sat (lunch), Sun and Mon. Moderate.*

Le Chapeau Melon

Olivier Camus runs the "Bowler Hat" in the Belleville neighborhood (not too far from the Parc des Buttes-Chaumont). This cozy place is primarily a shop featuring a large organic selection of wines. Evenings it becomes a restaurant serving a four-course (no-choice) menu for about €30. Casual, friendly, and worth the trip. *Info: 19th/Métro Pyrenées or Belleville. 92 rue Rébeval (at rue Rampal, off of rue de Belleville). Tel. 01/42.02.68.60. Open for dinner Wed-Sun. Wine shop Tue-Sat 11am-1pm and 4pm-8pm. Closed Mon. Moderate.*

Quedubon

Join the neighborhood locals at this wine bar, wine shop, and bistro located near the Parc des Buttes-Chaumont. You'll choose from a list of inexpensive, organic wines from the ever-changing chalkboard. Loved the farm chicken with braised endive. Excellent and large platter of *charcuterie*. *Info: 19th/Métro Buttes Chaumont. 22 Rue du Plateau (off of rue Botzaris). Tel. 01/42.38.18.65. Close Sat (lunch), Sun (dinner), and Mon. Inexpensive-Moderate.*

Roseval

This unpretentious restaurant in the Menilmontant neighborhood features delicious dining from chefs Simone Tondo and Michael Greenwold (who have left behind their former "fancy" posts). Prices are higher than you would find in the neighborhood, but you won't mind. The restaurant takes its name from *roseval* potatoes (a long, oval potato grown in France). The specialty is a puree of *roseval* potatoes with sautéed onions, clams, and a garnish of buttered bread crumbs. *Info: 20th/Métro Menilmontant. 1rue d'Eupatoria (at rue Julien-Lacroix, off of rue de Ménilmontant). Tel. 09/53.56.24.14. Open Mon-Fri (dinner only). Closed Sat and Sun. Moderate-Expensive.*

Ô Divin

Years ago, we visited this neighborhood to dine at the restaurant of chef Erik Frechon (who is now at the restaurant in the elegant Hôtel Le Bristol) and weren't disappointed. Now you can make the journey here for a lovely dining experience. This small and casual wine bar near the Parc des Buttes- Chaumont offers a large selection of organic wines. The menu is limited, but you won't be disappointed. And all at prices you won't find in wine bars in more touristy areas of Paris. *Info: 19th/Métro Botzaris. 35 rue des Annelets (off of rue de Crimée). Tel. 01/40.40.79.41. Closed Sun and Mon. Inexpensive-Moderate.*

Le Baratin

Locals and tourists are making the journey to this simple restaurant to taste the dishes of Argentinian-born chef Raquel Carena. The three-course lunch menu at less than €20 is a good value. Excellent rabbit stew and tuna carpaccio. The interesting wine list includes many organic choices. Don't be put off by the chef's gruff husband who manages the restaurant (although he is quite knowledgeable about wine). *Info: 20ᵗʰ/Métro Pyrenées. 3 rue Jouye-Rouve (off rue de Belleville). Tel 01/43.49.39.70. Closed Sun, Mon, Sat (lunch), and part of Aug. Moderate-Expensive.*

5. PRACTICAL MATTERS

GETTING TO PARIS
Airports/Arrival

Paris has two international airports: **Charles de Gaulle (Roissy)** and **Orly**. An Air France shuttle operates between the airports every 30 minutes. The trip takes up to 75 minutes and costs €18.

At Charles de Gaulle, a free shuttle bus connects **Aérogare 1** (used by most foreign carriers) with **Aérogare 2** (used primarily by Air France). This bus also drops you off at the Roissy train station. You can also walk through the terminals to the train station (just follow the signs). Once you get to the train station, skip attempting to use the self-service ticket kiosks (they frequently don't work with US credit cards). Just get in line at the ticket office. Your ticket is good for a transfer from the train to the metro system. **Line RER B** departs every 15 minutes from 5:30am to midnight to major métro stations. The cost is €9.25. Connecting métro lines will take you to your final destination. The train stops at Gare du Nord, Châtelet-Les Halles, St-Michel and Luxembourg stations. The trip takes about 35 minutes to Châtelet-Les Halles. By the way, keep your ticket. You need it to enter and exit the train stations.

The **Roissy buses** run every 15 minutes to and from the bus stop at Opéra Garnier on rue Scribe (€10, about a one-hour trip). You can reach your final destination by taking the métro from the nearby Opéra métro station.

A taxi ride costs at least €50 to the city center. The price will be a bit higher than on the meter as a charge will be added for your baggage. At night, fares are up to 50% higher. You'll find the taxi line outside the terminals. It will frequently be long, but moves quite fast. Never take an unmetered taxi! Minivan shuttles cost from €38 for two (shared ride). One service is

Parishutlle, *www.paris-shuttle.com, Tel. 877-404-9674 (from the US and Canada).*

Orly has two terminals: **Sud** (south) for international flights, and **Ouest** (west) for domestic flights. A free shuttle bus connects the two. A taxi from Orly to the city costs about €50 and up to 50% more at night. A bus to central Paris costs €9.

Orly Val is a monorail (stopping at both terminals) to the RER train station at Anthony (a ten-minute ride), then on to the city on the RER (Line B) train. The ride takes 35 minutes. The cost is €10.90 for both the monorail and the train ride.

GETTING AROUND PARIS
Car Rental
Are you crazy? Parking is chaotic, gas is extremely expensive, and driving in Paris is an unpleasant "adventure." With the incredible public transportation system in Paris, there's absolutely no reason to rent a car. If you do intend to drive, all major car rental companies have offices at both airports.

Métro (Subway)
The métro system is clearly the best way to get around Paris. It's orderly, inexpensive and for the most part safe. You're rarely far follow the line that your stop is on and note the last stop (the last stop appears on all the signs) and you'll soon be scurrying about underground like a Parisian. Service starts at 5:20am and ends at 1:20am (one additional hour on Saturday night/ Sunday mornings and the eve of holidays). Métro tickets are also valid on buses. Each ticket costs €1.70. Buy a *carnet* (10 tickets for €13.30). *www.ratp.fr*. If you buy a ticket on the bus, the cost is €2. Some métro stations have information desks and most have machines where you can purchase your tickets (and most machines now have instructions in English).

If you're staying in Paris for a longer period of time, a *carte navigo* for zones 1 and 2 (Paris and nearby suburbs) costs about €20 (plus a one-time fee of €5) a week or about €65 per month and allows unlimited use of both the métro and the bus system. You'll need a pass (you can get them at any major métro station) and a passport-size photo. That's why there are so many of those photo booths at stations. There are many options available for métro passes. Check them out. Keep your ticket throughout your trip. An inspector can fine you if you can't produce a stamped ticket.

Buses

Buses run from 5:30am to midnight, with some night routes running through the night. Bus routes are shown on the *Plan des Autobus*, a map available at métro stations. The route is shown at each bus stop. You can use métro tickets on the bus, but you can't switch between the bus and métro on the same ticket. Enter through the front door and validate your ticket in the machine behind the driver. You can also purchase a ticket from the driver. Exit out the back door.

If you'd like a quick tour of major sights, **bus #69** will take you from the Eiffel Tower (bus stop: Rapp-La Bourdonnais) passing the Seine River, the Louvre, through the Marais all the way to Père Lachaise Cemetery.

Taxis

You'll pay a minimum of €5 for a taxi ride. Fares are usually described in English on a sticker on the window. A typical 10-minute ride will cost around €10. There are taxi stands around the city, often near métro stops. Taxis G7 has a dedicated line for requests in English. *Call 01/41.27.66.99.*

BASIC INFORMATION

Banking & Changing Money

The **euro (€)** is the currency of France and most of Europe. Before you leave for Paris, it's a good idea to get some euros. It makes your arrival a lot easier. Call your credit-card company or bank before you leave to tell them that you'll be using your ATM or credit card outside the country. Many have automatic controls that can "freeze" your account if the computer program determines that there are charges outside your normal area. ATMs (of course, with fees) are the easiest way to change money in Paris. You'll find them everywhere. You can still get traveler's checks, but why bother?

Business Hours

Shop hours vary, but generally are from 9:30am to 7:30pm from Monday through Saturday. Most shops are closed on Sunday. Many restaurants and shops close for the month of August.

Climate& Weather

Average high temperature/low temperature/days of rain:
- January: 43° F / 34° F / 10
- February: 45° / 34° / 9
- March: 51° / 38° / 10
- April: 57° / 42° / 9
- May: 64° / 48°/ 10
- June: 70° /54° / 9
- July: 75°/ 58° / 8
- August: 75° / 57° / 7
- September: 69° / 52° / 9
- October: 59° / 46° / 10
- November: 49° / 39° / 10
- December: 45° / 36° / 11

Check *www.weather.com* before you leave.

Consulates & Embassies

- US: *8th/Métro Concorde, 2 ave. Gabriel, Tel. 01/43.12.22.22*
- Canada: *8th/Métro Franklin-D. Roosevelt, 35 avenue Montaigne, Tel. 01/44.43.29.00*

Electricity

The electrical current in Paris is **220 volts** as opposed to 110 volts found at home. Don't fry your electric razor, hairdryer or laptop. You'll need a converter and an adapter. (Most laptops don't require a converter, but why are you bringing that anyway?)

Emergencies & Safety

Paris is one of the safest large cities in the world. Still, don't wear a "fanny pack;" it's a sign that you're a tourist and an easy target (especially in crowded tourist areas and the métro). Avoid wearing expensive jewelry in the métro.

Insurance

Check with your health-care provider. Most policies don't cover you overseas. If that's the case, you may want to obtain medical insurance. Given the uncertainties in today's world, you may also want to purchase trip-cancellation insurance (for insurance coverage, check out www.insuremytrip.com). Make sure that your policy covers sickness, disasters, bankruptcy and State

Department travel restrictions and warnings. In other words, read the fine print!

Festivals

• **January**: If you love shopping, it's time for post-holiday bargains. Parisians call it *les soldes*. Paris is also host to the international ready-to-wear fashion shows held at the Parc des Expositions (15th).

• **February**: The *Salon de l'Agriculture* showcases France's important agricultural industry. Included in the celebration are food and wine from throughout France.

• **March**: At the end of the month is the F*oire du Trône*, a huge amusement park held at the Bois de Vincennes (12th). With Ferris wheels, circus attractions and carousels, it's like a sophisticated county fair.

• **April**: Paris is home to the International Marathon. On the first weekend, spectators line the Champs-Élysées to watch the women's and men's marathons. Events and concerts featuring jazz artists are held throughout the city.

• **May**: Tennis is king in late May as Paris hosts the French Open (they call it *Roland Garros*).

• **June**: Music fills the air during the many concerts as part of the *Fête de la Musique*. From Guatemalan street musicians to serious opera, you'll be exposed to Paris's diversity. Most concerts are free. Some of the best jazz artists come to Paris in June and July for the Paris Jazz Fest. Events and concerts are held in the Parc Floral (Bois de Vincennes).

• **July**: In early July, Paris hosts a huge gay-pride parade. On the 14th, Parisians celebrate *Le Quatorze Juillet* or Bastille Day with city-wide celebrations, fireworks and a huge military parade down the Champs-Élysées. In late July, the *Tour de France* is completed when bikers ride down the Champs-Élysées. This is also a huge month for *soldes* (clothing sales).

• **August**: Sunbathe, drink and celebrate the Seine River at *Paris-Plage*. Hundreds of deck chairs, umbrellas, cabanas and even palm trees are all brought to the Right Bank of the river from Pont de Sully to Pont Neuf. You can enjoy the sun, have a drink or two and a snack. No, I don't recommend that you swim in the Seine. In the late afternoon and evening, musicians play along the river.

• **September**: You can visit historical monuments (some of which are usually closed to the public) during *Fête du Patrimoine*. In late September, Paris again hosts the international ready-to-wear fashion convention at Parc des Expositions (15th).

• **October**: Thousands of horse-racing fans arrive in Paris for the *Prix de l'Arc de Triomphe Lucien Barrière*. It's considered to be the ultimate thoroughbred horse race. It's held at the Hippodrome de Longchamps (16th).

• **November**: Only in France would the arrival of wine be celebrated as a huge event. Get ready to drink Beaujolais Nouveau (a fruity wine from Burgundy) on the third Thursday.

• **December**: A skating rink is installed in front of the Hôtel de Ville (City Hall). The large windows of the major department stores (Bon Marché, BHV, Galeries Lafayette and Printemps) are decorated in interesting (sometimes bizarre) Christmas themes. *Fête de St-Sylvestre* (New Year's Eve) is celebrated throughout the city. At midnight, the Eiffel Tower is a virtual light show and the city is filled with champagne-drinking Parisians welcoming the new year (and a few tourists hoping they'll return to this great city in the years to come).

Holidays
• New Year's: January 1
• Easter
• Ascension (40 days after Easter)
• Pentecost (seventh Sunday after Easter)
• May Day: May 1
• Victory in Europe: May 8
• Bastille Day: July 14
• Assumption of the Virgin Mary: August 15
• All Saints': November 1
• Armistice: November 11
• Christmas: December 25

Internet Access

Cyber cafés seem to pop up everywhere (and go out of business quickly). You shouldn't have difficulty finding a place to e-mail home. Remember that French keyboards are different than those found in the U.S. and Canada. The going rate is about €3 per hour.

Language

Please, make the effort to speak a little French. It will get you a long way — even if all you can say is *Parlez-vous anglais?* (par-lay voo ahn-glay): Do you speak English? When you first speak to the salesperson in a shop or anyone else for that matter, always begin with a friendly *Bonjour* or *Bonsoir* (if it's evening). Gone are the days when Parisians were only interested in correcting your French. You'll find helpful French phrases on pages 122-123.

Packing

Never pack prescription drugs, eyeglasses or valuables. Carry them on. Think black. It always works for men and women. Oh, and by the way, pack light. Don't ruin your trip by having to lug around huge suitcases. Before you leave home, make copies of your passport, airline tickets and confirmation of hotel reservations. You should also make a list of your credit-card numbers and the telephone numbers for your credit-card companies. If you lose any of them (or they're stolen), you can call someone at home and have them provide the information to you. You should also pack copies of these documents separate from the originals.

Passport Regulations

You'll need a valid passport to enter France. If you're staying more than 90 days, you must obtain a visa. Canadians don't need visas.

Citizens of the U.S. who have been away more than 48 hours can bring home $800 of merchandise duty-free every 30 days. For more information, go to Traveler Information ("Know Before You Go") at *www.customs.gov.* Canadians can bring back C$750 each year if gone for 7 days or more.

Hotel and restaurant prices are required by law to include taxes and service charges. **Value Added Tax** (VAT, or TVA in French) is nearly 20% (higher on luxury goods). The VAT is included in the price of goods (except services such as restaurants). Foreigners are entitled to a refund and must fill out a refund form. When you make your purchase, ask for the form and instructions if you're purchasing €175 or more in one place and in one day (no combining). Yes, it can be a hassle. Check out *www.global-blue.com* or *www.premiertaxfree.com* for the latest information on refunds (and help for a fee).

Postal Services

Be prepared to wait in line. There is a post office at 52 rue du Louvre that's open 24 hours. If you're mailing postcards, you can purchase stamps at many *tabacs* (tobacco shops) and stands that sell newspapers and postcards.

Restrooms

There aren't a lot of public restrooms. If you need to go, your best bet is to head (no pun intended) to the nearest café or brasserie. It's considered good manners to purchase something if you use the restroom. Some métro stations have public restrooms. Another option are those strange self-cleaning restrooms that look like some sort of pod found on some streets in Paris (they are free); there is one at the bottom of the hill before you climb up the stairs to Sacré-Coeur in Montmartre. Don't be shocked to walk into a restroom and find two porcelain foot prints and a hole in the floor. These old "Turkish toilets" still exist. Hope you have strong thighs!

Smoking

There is now a smoking ban for all public places. Beginning in 2008, restaurants, hotels, bars-tabacs, and nightclubs must be smoke-free. If it can happen in Paris, it can happen anywhere. You can still smoke at outdoor cafés.

Telephones
- Country code for France is 33
- Area code for Paris is 01
- Calls beginning with 0800 are toll-free
- Calling Paris from the U.S. and Canada: dial 011-33-1 plus the eight-digit local number. You drop the 0 in the area code
- Calling the U.S. or Canada from Paris: dial 00 (wait for the tone), dial 1 plus the area code and local number
- Calling within Paris: dial 01 and the eight-digit local number.

Phone cards are the cheapest way to call. Get one from many tabacs or magazine kiosks.

A great way to stay in touch and save money is to rent an **international cell phone**. One provider is *www.cellhire.com*. Few cell phones purchased in the U.S. work in Europe. If you're a frequent visitor to Europe, you may want to purchase a cell phone (for about $50) from *www.mobal.com*. You'll get an international telephone number and pay by the minute for calls made on your cell phone. If you are using a smartphone in Paris, make sure to turn off your international roaming (and use WiFi instead) to save a lot of money.

Time
When it's noon in New York City, it's 6pm in Paris. For hours of events or schedules, the French use the 24-hour clock. So 6am is 0600 and 1pm is 1300.

Tipping
See Chapter 2 (page 17) for tipping in restaurants. Other tips: 10% for taxi drivers, €1 for room service, €1.50 per bag to the hotel porter, €1.50 per day for maid service and up to €50 to bathroom attendants.

Tourist Information
There are tourist information offices at both airports and at the following locations: 25 rue des Pyramides (1st/Métro Pyramides): Open daily 9am-7pm (winter 10am-7pm); Gare de Lyon train station (12th/Métro Gare de Lyon): Open Mon-Sat 8am-6pm, closed Sun; Gare du Nord train station (10th/Métro Gare du Nord: Open daily 8am-6pm; 72 blvd. Rochechouart (18th/Métro Anvers): Open daily 10am-6pm; Corner of Champs-Élysées and Ave. de Marigney (8th/Metro Champs-Élysées-Clémenceau): Open daily 10am-7pm (late May to mid-October).

Water
Tap water is safe in Paris. Occasionally, you'll find *non potable* signs in restrooms. This means that the water is not safe for drinking.

Web Sites
• Open Road Travel Guides: www.openroadguides.com
• Author's website: www.eatndrink.com
• Paris Tourist Office: www.parisinfo.com
• French Government Tourist Office: www.franceguide.com
• U.S. State Department: www.state.gov

ESSENTIAL FRENCH PHRASES

please, *s'il vous plait* (seel voo play)
thank you, *merci* (mair see)
yes, *oui* (wee)
no, *non* (nohn)
good morning, *bonjour* (bohn jhoor)
good afternoon, *bonjour* (bohn jhoor)
good evening, *bonsoir* (bohn swahr)
goodbye, *au revoir* (o ruh vwahr)
sorry/excuse me, *pardon* (pahr-dohn)
you are welcome, *de rien* (duh ree ehn)

do you speak English?, *parlez-vous anglais?* (par lay voo ahn glay)
I don't speak French, *je ne parle pas français* (jhuh ne parl pah frahn say)
I don't understand, *je ne comprends pas* (jhuh ne kohm prahn pas)
I'd like a table, *je voudrais une table* (zhuh voo dray ewn tabl)
I'd like to reserve a table, *je voudrais réserver une table* (zhuh voo dray rayzehrvay ewn tabl)
for one, *pour un* (poor oon), two, *deux* (duh), *trois* (twah)(3), *quatre* (kaht-ruh)(4), *cinq* (sank)(5), *six* (cease)(6), *sept* (set)(7), *huit* (wheat)(8), *neuf* (nerf)(9), *dix* (dease)(10)
waiter/sir, *monsieur* (muh-syuh) (never garçon!)
waitress/miss, *mademoiselle* (mad mwa zel)
knife, *couteau* (koo toe)
spoon, *cuillère* (kwee air)
fork, *fourchette* (four shet)
menu, *la carte* (la cart) (not menu!)
wine list, *la carte des vins* (la cart day van)
no smoking, *défense de fumer* (day fahns de fu may)
toilets, *les toilettes* (lay twa lets)

closed, *fermé* (fehr-may)
open, *ouvert* (oo-vehr)
today, *aujourd'hui* (o zhoor dwee)
tomorrow, *demain* (duh mehn)
tonight, *ce soir* (suh swahr)
Monday, *lundi* (luhn dee)
Tuesday, *mardi* (mahr dee)
Wednesday, *mercredi* (mair kruh dee)

Thursday, *jeudi* (jheu dee)
Friday, *vendredi* (vawn druh dee)
Saturday, *samedi* (sahm dee)
Sunday, *dimanche* (dee mahnsh)

here, *ici* (ee-see)
there, *là* (la)
what, *quoi* (kwah)
when, *quand* (kahn)
where, *où est* (ooh-eh)
how much, *c'est combien* (say comb bee ehn)
credit cards, *les cartes de crédit* (lay kart duh creh dee)

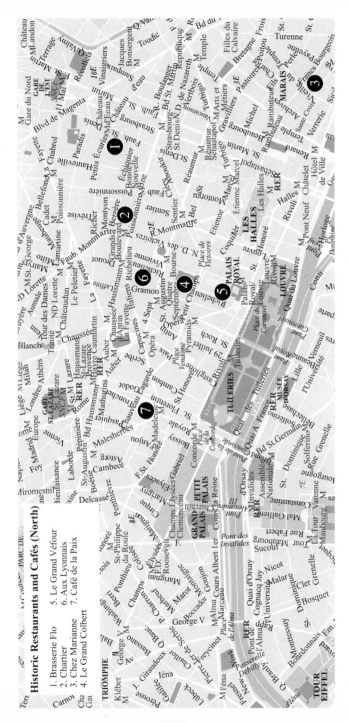

Historic Restaurants and Cafés (North)

1. Brasserie Flo
2. Chartier
3. Chez Marianne
4. Le Grand Colbert
5. Le Grand Véfour
6. Aux Lyonnais
7. Café de la Paix

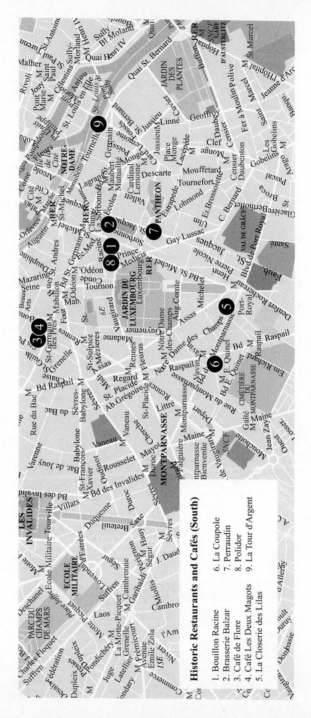

Historic Restaurants and Cafés (South)

1. Bouillon Racine
2. Brasserie Balzar
3. Café de Flore
4. Café Les Deux Magots
5. La Closerie des Lilas
6. La Coupole
7. Perraudin
8. Polidor
9. La Tour d'Argent

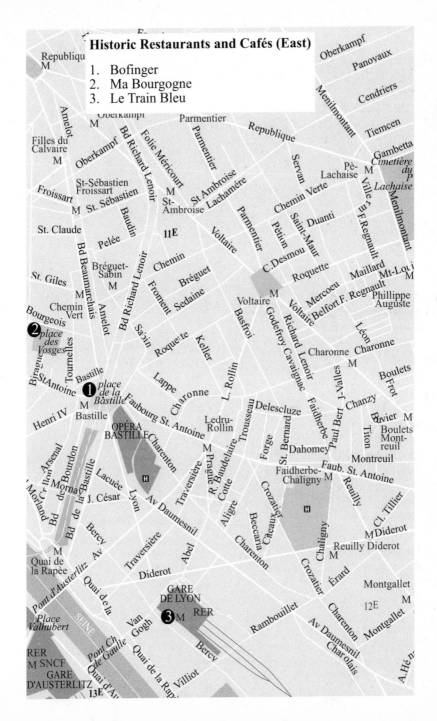

Historic Restaurants and Cafés (East)

1. Bofinger
2. Ma Bourgogne
3. Le Train Bleu

INDEX

Note: see "Places to Wine and Dine by Arrondissement" for individual restaurant and wine bar listings beginning at the bottom of page 130.

INDEX

Places to Wine and Dine by Arrondissement

INDEX

Acknowledgments

Wining and Dining in Paris would not have been possible without the help of Jonathan Stein of Open Road Publishing.

Christine Humphrey, founder and editor of *Grapegazette.com*, wrote the chapter on French wines.

Trish and Terry Medalen found many of the restaurants and wine bars in this book.

Editor: Marian Modesta Olson.
Illustrations by Michael Dillon of McDill Design.

About the Authors

Andy Herbach is the author of the Eating & Drinking series of menu translators and restaurant guides, including *Eating & Drinking in Paris, Eating & Drinking in Italy*, and *Eating & Drinking in Spain and Portugal*. He is also the author of several Open Road guides, including *Open Road's Best of Paris* and *Open Road's Best of Provence and the French Riviera*.

Karl Raaum is a contributor to the Eating & Drinking and Open Road's Best Of guides. He has also contributed to guides to Amsterdam and Berlin.

The authors reside in Palm Springs, California.

You can e-mail the authors corrections, additions, and comments at *eatndrink@aol.com* or through *www.eatndrink.com*.

Photo Credits

Front cover: Phyllis Flick/myparisnotebook.com; back cover: Christine Humphrey/grapegazette.com; page 7: Chris Friese at flickr.com; page 14: Zdenko Zivkovic at flickr.com.

COMMENTS PLEASE

We enjoy getting feedback, positive or not, so please let us know if you agree or disagree with anything in our book. No item is too small, so please send us your thoughts. E-mail us at: eatndrink@aol.com.